S0-BBV-340

SAT Reading - Yellow

Homework: Version 1.3

C2 Education is a registered trademark of C2 Educational Center, Inc.

This publication is designed to provide accurate and authoritative information in regard to the subject matter covered. It is sold with the understanding that the publisher is not engaged in rendering legal, accounting, or other professional service. If legal advice or other expert assistance is required, the services of a competent professional should be sought.

© 2013 by Reetiforp, LLC. All rights reserved. Printed in the United States of America. Except as permitted under the United States Copyright Act of 1976, no part of this publication may be reproduced or distributed in any form or by any means, or stored in a data base or retrieval system, without the prior written permission of the publisher.

Published by Reetiforp, LLC Publishing, a division of Reetiforp, LLC

Reetiforp Publishing books are available at special quantity discounts to use for sales promotions, employee premiums, or educational purposes. Please email our Marketing Department to order or for more information at c2educate@c2educate.com. Please report any errors or corrections to c2tutors@c2educate.com.

SAT Reading Yellow: Table of Contents

Y1HW: Homework and Extra Practice

SC TOPIC: Introduction	RC TOPIC: Active Reading (Lesson Y1b)

Homework Set 1

1. Marjorie's performance in the play received great ------, as several reviewers said that she deserved to win an award.

   (A) contradiction
   (B) criticism
   (C) omission
   (D) discontent
   (E) acclaim

2. Although Lao claimed that his mistake had been ------, many of his friends thought that it must have been on purpose.

   (A) intentional
   (B) reckless
   (C) competent
   (D) deliberate
   (E) inadvertent

3. Rather than use traditional methods to grow his crops, the farmer sought out ------ solutions to increase his production.

   (A) preoccupied
   (B) stale
   (C) absurd
   (D) erratic
   (E) innovative

4. After the car crash, Anna felt ------ at first but was soon able to think clearly again.

   (A) enthusiastic
   (B) rational
   (C) gratified
   (D) dazed
   (E) industrious

5. Roger was a ------ figure in his hometown, but he quickly realized that the people in the big city did not know him, and many of them dismissed his small-town ways as being ------.

   (A) cryptic . . coarse
   (B) superficial . . refined
   (C) distinguished . . cultured
   (D) prominent . . unsophisticated
   (E) frivolous . . primitive

6. After dropping his glasses in the lake, Lamar searched for them, but he could not find them because they were ------ by the ------ water.

   (A) flourished . . luminous
   (B) obscured . . murky
   (C) exhibited . . flawless
   (D) imparted . . righteous
   (E) veiled . . transparent

a word or phrase implying 'non-traditional' Regulary, normally

 Unauthorized copying or reuse of any part of this page is illegal.

Homework Set 2

7. The reporter suspected that the mayor was not being ------ with her, so she pressed for a more complete and honest answer.

    (A) simplistic
    (B) deceitful
    (C) inconsiderate
    (D) cowardly
    (E) forthright

8. In order to ------ his goal of becoming a lawyer, Julio had to complete law school and pass the bar exam.

    (A) consume
    (B) suppress
    (C) negate
    (D) attain
    (E) discount

9. Many of Paula's co-workers were offended by her ------ humor, so her boss ------ her and told her to stop.

    (A) upright . . scolded
    (B) vile . . glorified
    (C) impartial . . overlooked
    (D) invigorating . . astonished
    (E) crude . . reprimanded

10. The song was ------ a bygone era, and caused many who heard it to remember people and events that they had not thought of for decades.

    (A) irrelevant to
    (B) hideous to
    (C) evocative of
    (D) distressed by
    (E) resentful of

11. Sarah was very ------ about her duties as hostess, and went out of her way to ------ every guest so that no one would feel left out.

    (A) lenient . . socialize with
    (B) diligent . . mingle with
    (C) timid . . thrash
    (D) vague . . demolish
    (E) conscientious . . deflect

12. When writing an essay, it is important to know that while a ------, five-paragraph essay is likely to get a decent score, most truly outstanding essays are more unusual or creative.

    (A) fertile
    (B) abnormal
    (C) exquisite
    (D) conventional
    (E) bizarre

evocate: bring memories to mind

Conventional - usual or traditional

Unauthorized copying or reuse of any part of this page is illegal.

Homework Passage 1 (Short)

A man bites into a lemon wedge. He does not wince or complain. In fact, he seems not to be bothered at all by the citrus fruit's notorious sourness. Is this some sort of *Line* miracle? No—though it does involve so-called "miracle *(5)* berries." These fruits, which are native to western Africa, are tart when eaten but have a very peculiar after-effect: they make sour foods taste sweet. Thus, the lemon wedge that the man ate tasted much like a lemon drop candy. The effect lasts for up to an hour.

(10) Scientists are unsure about exactly how the miracle berry works. No other known substances can alter a person's sense of taste in this way. They theorize that perhaps the tongue's sweetness receptors are altered so that they respond to acids instead of sugars.

13. According to the passage, the man "does not wince or complain" (lines 1-2) because

   (A) he did not actually eat the lemon wedge.
   (B) a miracle allowed him to enjoy sour flavors.
   (C) the miracle berries made the lemon wedge taste sweet instead of sour.
   (D) the lemon that he ate was a new variety that has been bred to taste less sour.
   (E) his tongue lacks the ability to taste sourness.

14. The primary purpose of the passage is to

   (A) convince the reader to eat more lemons.
   (B) contrast lemons and miracle berries.
   (C) explain the process by which the body processes different tastes.
   (D) describe an unusual property of a particular food.
   (E) provide an example of a real-life miracle.

Homework Passage 2 (Short)

Many popular musicians and singers have died at an early age, from Buddy Holly and Jimi Hendrix to Kurt Cobain and Tupac Shakur. Perhaps none of these deaths *Line* was as tragic as the death of the Mexican-American *(5)* singer and songwriter known as Selena, who was fatally shot—at the age of only 23—by the former president of her fan club.

At the time of her death in 1994, Selena had already sold millions of albums worldwide, but she was not very *(10)* well known outside of the Spanish-speaking community. She was working on her first English-language album when she died, an album which promised to be her most successful yet.

Sadly, Selena's greatest success came after her *(15)* murder. When her final album, *Dreaming of You*, came out a few months after her death, it set many sales records, including the most copies sold in a single day by a female pop singer and the most total copies sold by a Hispanic artist. In addition, a movie about her life came *(20)* out in 1997, starring Jennifer Lopez as Selena.

15. Which of the following would make the best title for the passage?

   (A) The Triumph of Selena
   (B) A History of Singers Who Died Tragically
   (C) Bilingual American Entertainers
   (D) A Star Who Died Before Her Time
   (E) The Dangers of Being a Pop Star

16. The success of Selena's "final album" (line 15) can best be described as

   (A) bittersweet.
   (B) ordinary.
   (C) resentful.
   (D) joyous.
   (E) substandard.

    Unauthorized copying or reuse of any part of this page is illegal.

Homework Passage 3 (Short)

The Red Cross, which today is one of the largest and most respected charities in the world, serves to aid the victims of war and natural disasters as well as to help
Line prepare communities for these events. This huge
(5) organization began with the work of just one woman, the pioneering American nurse Clara Barton. Barton was the first woman to serve as a nurse on the front lines of a major war (the U.S. Civil War). After witnessing the horrors of the war first-hand, she sought to create an
(10) organization that would help injured soldiers and others in need of emergency medical care. In 1881, she successfully lobbied President James Garfield to found the first chapter of the American Red Cross and began serving as its first president. This accomplishment was
(15) made all the more extraordinary by the fact that women would not even be allowed to vote in America for another 29 years. Barton would serve as the organization's president until 1904, when she retired at the age of 83.

17. What motivated Clara Barton to "create an organization that would help injured soldiers" (lines 9-10)?

   (A) a plea from President Garfield
   (B) hearing stories of terrible battlefield conditions
   (C) her experiences as a nurse in the Civil War
   (D) her disregard for the abilities of most doctors
   (E) a deadly hurricane

18. According to the passage, Barton's achievements are particularly impressive because she

   (A) died at an early age.
   (B) overcame an early-life disability.
   (C) foresaw the horrors of the Civil War.
   (D) worked independently, not seeking the help of any powerful figures.
   (E) accomplished so much in an era when women were not treated as equal to men.

Homework Passage 4 (Long)

The following passage is an excerpt from a 1995 essay on the importance of volunteerism in a democracy.

Effective democracy requires a healthy balance between civic rights and obligations. Most Americans appear to be well informed of and eager to protect their
Line civic rights, but too many lack commitment to their civic
(5) obligations for the proper functioning of a constitutional democracy.

In recent decades, there has been a disturbing decline in the willingness of America's youth to participate in service to the community or nation. According to "People
(10) for the American Way," there are five major reasons why young Americans are reluctant to serve.

The first is lack of time. Students complain that too many demands are placed on them, such as competing for good grades, needs for after-school jobs, athletic
(15) commitments, and family obligations, which leave little time for other endeavors. A second reason often cited by students is the lack of parental encouragement. When parents do not have time to devote to Boy Scouts, community projects, or the American Heart Association,
(20) their children do not have role models for civic service. We are often asking students to perform services that are beyond their realm of experience and therefore completely foreign to them. According to some experts, however, perhaps the greatest reason is that we simply do
(25) not ask young people to get involved. We incorrectly assume that youngsters will seek opportunities to serve and disregard their need to be invited.

The final two reasons identified by this study involve the perceptions of youth toward democracy.
(30) Many young Americans do not understand the obligations of the citizen in a democratic society. They are well aware of their personal rights and freedoms, but are sadly ignorant of their duties. Finally, most youth have too little faith in our political institutions and
(35) leaders and in their ability to bring about positive change.

Morris Janowitz takes a slightly different approach to the question of why youngsters are reluctant to serve by suggesting that most have been conditioned to act on their own narrow self-interests. They perceive national
(40) and community service as contrary to their own personal economic goals and as a restrictive environment that infringes upon their quest for personal pleasure. Civic education must work to reaffirm the beliefs of young Americans that self-interests are always deeply rooted in
(45) community and nation, and that serving one's nation and community also serves oneself.

Unauthorized copying or reuse of any part of this page is illegal.

Version 1.3

19. According to the author of the passage, what "disturbing" (line 7) trend has occurred in recent years?

    (A) a reduction in the amount of faith American citizens have in their government
    (B) a rise in students' need for having after-school jobs
    (C) a decline in community service, particularly among young people
    (D) a decrease in citizenship test scores
    (E) an increase in competitiveness among young people

20. In context, the word "foreign" (line 23) most nearly means

    (A) from another country.
    (B) bizarre.
    (C) irrelevant.
    (D) unknown.
    (E) illegal.

21. According to the passage, what can parents do to encourage their children to be more active in community service?

    (A) serve as a role model by finding time for themselves to volunteer
    (B) place a greater emphasis on getting good grades
    (C) tell children that since the government is ineffective, communities must pick up the slack
    (D) inform children of their civic rights
    (E) emphasize the importance of family obligations

22. Which of the following does the passage NOT identify as an explanation for the decline in youth volunteering?

    (A) Students do not understand the obligations of being a citizen of a democracy.
    (B) Young people do not think that they can make a difference.
    (C) Youths do not have enough free time to volunteer.
    (D) All students are immoral and selfish.
    (E) Young people are not asked to volunteer.

23. According to Morris Janowitz (line 36), the best way to encourage students to volunteer more is to

    (A) require all students to perform community service.
    (B) reward volunteering with scholarships or greater freedoms.
    (C) make sure they have plenty of free time.
    (D) convince them that what is good for their nation and community is also good for them.
    (E) punish those who do not volunteer.

24. The primary purpose of this passage is to

    (A) criticize young people for being lazy.
    (B) encourage students to focus less on getting good grades and more on being a good citizen.
    (C) praise young people for acting in their own self interest.
    (D) point out that a lack of volunteerism has not harmed our democracy.
    (E) outline some of the factors that have contributed to a growing problem.

Unauthorized copying or reuse of any part of this page is illegal.

6

SC TOPIC: Using C2's 5-Step Method (Lesson Y2a)	**RC TOPIC**: Active Reading (Lesson Y1b)

Homework Set 1

1. To Gene's ------, he was unable to find his favorite tie, forcing him to wear a less fashionable one.

   (A) dismay
   (B) delight
   (C) endurance
   (D) credit
   (E) charity

2. Although the investigators ------ that the witness was telling the truth, they were unwilling to admit that he had revealed everything, and so they remained ------ his answers.

   (A) contended . . gullible about
   (B) conceded . . skeptical of
   (C) granted . . authentic about
   (D) quarreled . . inattentive to
   (E) disputed . . leery of

3. The ------ inventor wore an unusual outfit that resembled a clown suit and had a huge, ------ mass of unruly grey hair.

   (A) conventional . . chaotic
   (B) peculiar . . precise
   (C) commonplace . . tame
   (D) evocative . . systematic
   (E) eccentric . . snarled

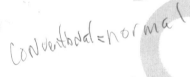

4. Though she was denied entry to her preferred college at first, Rosa ------, and on her fourth attempt, she was accepted.

   (A) abandoned
   (B) persisted
   (C) succumbed
   (D) withdrew
   (E) ceased

5. The professor offered his students a choice: do a 5-minute presentation on one's own, or ------ another student on a 10-minute presentation.

   (A) acclaim
   (B) collaborate with
   (C) forbid
   (D) refrain from
   (E) flee from

6. The reaction to the city council's plan was largely ------, with over a thousand citizens lining up outside city hall to protest the plan.

   (A) fond
   (B) sympathetic
   (C) ecstatic
   (D) hostile
   (E) sentimental

Unauthorized copying or reuse of any part of this page is illegal.

Version 1.3

Homework Set 2

7. The artist's latest statue was polarizing, with some ------ it to be spectacularly beautiful and others criticizing it as ugly and even ------.

   (A) proclaiming . . repulsive
   (B) extinguishing . . obnoxious
   (C) affirming . . enchanting
   (D) begrudging . . innovative
   (E) professing . . soothing

8. Though she endured many setbacks on her road to success, the author never lost her ------ that her books would one day be read and admired by people worldwide.

   (A) conviction
   (B) agitation
   (C) hesitation
   (D) disquiet
   (E) prominence

9. Fortunately for the nearby town, which was ------ a flood, the river ------ its dangerous level to one that was much less threatening.

   (A) ambiguous about . . subsided from
   (B) immune to . . propelled toward
   (C) vulnerable to . . receded from
   (D) sheltered from . . lurked within
   (E) susceptible to . . ascended from

10. The principal emphasized that although the students were not ------ to go to the pep rally, attendance was strongly encouraged.

    (A) discharged
    (B) assured
    (C) alleged
    (D) obligated
    (E) counseled

11. After the dog chewed up his homework, Hiram was unable to ------ the assignment and had to complete it all over again.

    (A) impair
    (B) salvage
    (C) corrupt
    (D) demote
    (E) trample

12. Afraid that her speech was too ------ to be given within the time limit, Soon-yi eliminated three paragraphs.

    (A) compact
    (B) profound
    (C) abrupt
    (D) verbose — lots or too many words
    (E) hasty

what is opposite of verbose?
succint (briefly ? clearly expressed

C2 education
be smarter.

Homework Passage 1 (Short)

The first human-made objects to leave our solar system, the Voyager I and Voyager II probes, both contain a curious payload: a golden record. These records
Line hold more than just a few catchy songs, though. Each
(5) record contains pictures, sounds, music, and other information designed to describe humanity and Earth to any alien civilization that might discover one of the probes. The gold records include spoken greetings in 55 languages, music from many cultures (including Chuck
(10) Berry's classic rock 'n roll song, "Johnny B. Goode"), and over 100 images of humans, animals, Earth, and the solar system. There is even a recording of a human heartbeat. The records are designed to be interpretable by aliens who know nothing of our cultures or languages,
(15) but it may take a while for us to find out if our message was received. Neither probe will reach the vicinity of another star for 40,000 years.

13. In context, the word "curious" (line 3) most nearly means

(A) expensive.
(B) nosy.
(C) inquisitive.
(D) questionable.
(E) odd.

14. Which of the following titles for the passage is most appropriate?

(A) Chuck Berry: America's Ambassador
(B) A Message to the Stars
(C) Seeing the Solar System from a New Angle
(D) What We Learned from the Voyager Probes
(E) Why We Will Talk to Aliens Soon

vicinity-area around a
particular place

Homework Passage 2 (Short)

Cab Calloway began singing in jazz clubs while he was still in high school in the early 1920s, and was still performing almost 70 years later, when he was in his
Line eighties. In between, his career was noteworthy not just
(5) for its length but also for its variety. In addition to popularizing the "scat" form of singing, which features jazz-like improvisation of nonsense syllables, Calloway led one of the most popular big bands of the 1930s and 1940s. He was also part of Bing Crosby's backup band
(10) on NBC radio (making Calloway the first African-American to appear on major broadcast radio). He was even a noted dancer, inventing a backward-slide move similar to Michael Jackson's famed "moonwalk"—50 years before Jackson first performed it.
(15)   Later in his career, Calloway starred in over a dozen movies, sang in several hit Broadway musicals, and wrote two books. He even appeared on *Sesame Street* (singing with the "Two-Headed Monster" muppet) and in a music video for Janet Jackson's hit song "Alright."
(20) These and other appearances reinforced Calloway's enduring appeal and introduced his music to new generations of listeners.

15. The author's tone when describing Calloway is most nearly

(A) egotistical.
(B) admiring.
(C) annoyed.
(D) neutral.
(E) dismissive.

16. Cab Calloway's career can best be described as which of the following?

(A) comedic.
(B) short-lived.
(C) unoriginal.
(D) wide-ranging.
(E) dull.

Unauthorized copying or reuse of any part of this page is illegal.   Version 1.3

Homework Passage 3 (Short)

Papua New Guinea is a diverse country of 4 million people and 800 languages. It is home to more than 200 cultures, each with its own traditions. Because 85 percent *Line* of Papua New Guinea consists of dense rain forest—and *(5)* because of its rough, mountainous terrain—many of its tribes seldom have contact with each other, and even more rarely interact with the outside world. For most people living in rural villages in Papua New Guinea, life goes on without change year after year. Traditions and *(10)* customs remain the same from one generation to the next. The tribal cultures are primarily communal ones in which each member of the community can count on being cared for in some way within a circle of family, community, and friends.

17. According to the passage, many villages in Papua New Guinea are

   (A) culturally distinct.
   (B) constantly varying.
   (C) anti-social.
   (D) dependent on other villages.
   (E) globally conscious.

18. The passage implies that Papua New Guinea is the source of so many languages and cultures primarily because

   (A) its citizens choose not to communicate with the world outside their village.
   (B) its geography greatly limits the impact that cultures can have on one another.
   (C) each culture is rapidly evolving.
   (D) all of its cultures possess a shared respect for diversity.
   (E) its tribes are primitive and closed-minded.

Homework Passage 4 (Long)

This passage is a brief history of some of the youngest people to have served in the United States Senate.

When the Senate convened on November 16, 1818, it set a record that is never likely to be broken. Members on that occasion, however, probably did not realize they *Line* were making history—and violating the Constitution—in *(5)* administering the oath of office to Tennessee's 28-year-old John Henry Eaton.

The framers of the Constitution set the minimum age for Senate service at 30 years. They arrived at that number by adding five years to the 25-year minimum *(10)* they had established for House members, reasoning that the deliberative nature of the "senatorial trust" called for a "greater extent of information and stability of character" than would be needed in the House.

Apparently no one asked John Eaton how old he *(15)* was. In those days of large families and poorly kept birth records, he may not have been able to answer that question. Perhaps it was only later that he determined the birth date that now appears on his tombstone, confirming his less-than-constitutional age. Had someone in 1818 *(20)* chosen to challenge his seating, Eaton could have pointed to the Senate's 1816 decision to seat Virginia's 28-year-old Armistead Mason, or the 1806 precedent to admit 29-year-old Henry Clay.

Within a few years of Eaton's swearing-in, the *(25)* Senate began to pay closer attention to such matters. This issue then lay dormant for more than a century until the 1934 election of Rush Holt, a 29-year-old West Virginia Democrat. During his campaign, Holt had pledged to wait six months into the 1935 session until his 30th *(30)* birthday to be sworn in. While he was waiting, his defeated Republican opponent, former incumbent Senator Henry Hatfield, filed a petition with the Senate charging that Holt's failure to meet the constitutional age requirement invalidated his election. Hatfield therefore *(35)* asked that he be declared the winner, having received the highest number of votes among other eligible candidates.

The Senate dismissed Hatfield's arguments, observing that the age requirement applies at the time of oath-taking rather than the time of election, or the time *(40)* the term begins. It also reiterated that the ineligibility of the winning candidate gives no title to the candidate receiving the next highest number of votes. On June 21, 1935, Holt followed in the line of Eaton, Mason, and Clay as the Senate's fourth youngest member, beating by *(45)* 28 days the fifth youngest member, William Wells of Delaware, who took the oath of office in 1799. In January 1973, the distinction of becoming the sixth youngest—and the youngest since Holt, at the age of 30 years, 1 month, and 14 days—went to Delaware's Joseph *(50)* Biden, who would one day become Vice-President.

deliberative
precedent
incumbent

Version 1.3   Unauthorized copying or reuse of any part of this page is illegal.

19. Why did the senators "probably not realize they were making history" (lines 3-4) on November 16, 1818?

 (A) They were unaware of the rule requiring senators to be at least 30 years old.
 (B) They did not realize that John Henry Eaton was only 28.
 (C) They were too busy worrying about more important issues.
 (D) They assumed that Eaton's oath would be challenged and that he would never be seated.
 (E) They thought that 28-year-old senators would be commonplace in the future.

20. According to the passage, what was the purpose of the Senate's age requirement?

 (A) to ensure that every senator was born before the signing of the Declaration of Independence
 (B) to restrict the office to those who had completed their college educations
 (C) to ensure that senators would have a certain amount of experience and maturity.
 (D) to provide a trivial difference between the House and the Senate.
 (E) to reduce the number of feuds and physical confrontations in the Senate chambers

21. According to the passage, what is the most likely reason that John Henry Eaton might "not have been able to" (line 16) say what his exact age was?

 (A) His parents lied to him about when he was born.
 (B) He was born in a foreign country.
 (C) His memory was very unreliable.
 (D) He was adopted.
 (E) There was not an accurate record of his birth date.

22. Based on information in the passage, why is it unlikely that the Senate will seat another 28-year-old in the future?

 (A) The Senate now pays much closer attention to the ages of its members.
 (B) The courts will not allow anyone to be elected to the Senate unless he or she is at least 30.
 (C) The Senate's minimum age has since been raised to 35.
 (D) People today are much less likely to lie about their age than people from the 19th century.
 (E) Young adults have no desire to serve in important government offices.

23. The story about the election of Rush Holt (lines 28-44) illustrates what important fact about the Senate?

 (A) The second-leading vote-getter is entitled to a Senate seat when the winner is ruled ineligible.
 (B) A senator's age at the time of election is less important than his or her age when taking the oath of office.
 (C) A senator-elect must take the oath of office at the same time as his or her colleagues.
 (D) Long-time incumbents have far more power than newly-elected senators.
 (E) A person must be at least 30 years old to be legally elected to the Senate.

24. In context, the word "distinction" (line 47) most nearly means

 (A) foul odor
 (B) significance
 (C) awkwardness
 (D) division
 (E) regularity

25. The primary purpose of this passage is to

 (A) criticize the 1818 Senate for violating the Constitution.
 (B) provide an outline of the debate over lowering the Senate's minimum age requirement to 25.
 (C) tell the life story of former senator Rush Holt.
 (D) list some of the youngest U.S. senators and describe how they have been seated.
 (E) illustrate the difficulties of providing accurate birth dates in the early 19th century.

Unauthorized copying or reuse of any part of this page is illegal.

Version 1.3

Y3HW: Homework and Extra Practice

SC TOPIC: Using C2's 5-Step Method (Lesson Y2a)	**RC TOPIC**: Synthesizing (Lesson Y3b)

Homework Set 1

1. After a week of waiting and no response, Daniel ------ his offer to take Sharita to the dance so that he could ask someone else.

   (A) persisted
   (B) retracted
   (C) supplemented
   (D) inflicted
   (E) corresponded

2. Logan ordered ten pizzas for the party at his house, but many of these proved to be ------ when only five people showed up.

   (A) crucial
   (B) habitual
   (C) superfluous
   (D) mandatory
   (E) conventional

3. Rosie's ------ decision to buy a lottery ticket may have been poorly thought-out, but it was also ------, for she won $20.

   (A) reluctant . . barren
   (B) spontaneous . . deficient
   (C) impulsive . . opportune
   (D) fanciful . . futile
   (E) prolonged . . fortuitous

4. The jewelry expert ------ the necklace and found that it was worth at least $1,000.

   (A) abolished
   (B) dispersed
   (C) appraised
   (D) neglected
   (E) severed

5. The ------ history of air travel included ------ of interesting facts and many stories about the first commercial airliners.

   (A) comprehensive . . a multitude
   (B) appealing . . a deficit
   (C) verbose . . a scarcity
   (D) lopsided . . an array
   (E) extensive . . a poverty

6. Although most people think of bacteria as being dangerous and harmful, in reality most types of bacteria are ------ or even helpful to humans.

   (A) repulsive
   (B) spiteful
   (C) benign
   (D) scandalous
   (E) nauseating

Unauthorized copying or reuse of any part of this page is illegal.

Homework Set 2

7. The judge ------ the proceedings by banging his gavel and ------, "court is now in session."

    (A) inferred . . acclaiming
    (B) undertook . . renouncing
    (C) terminated . . rustling
    (D) halted . . denouncing
    (E) initiated . . proclaiming

8. Since we cannot travel back in time, we can only ------ that the paintings and statues of historical figures are ------; we can never know for sure.

    (A) disown . . erroneous
    (B) suppose . . genuine
    (C) attain . . precise
    (D) consume . . authentic
    (E) surmise . . dreadful

9. In order to ------ the rule banning bottles with more than one ounce of liquid, Randy poured his soda into twelve one-ounce bottles.

    (A) collaborate
    (B) reinforce
    (C) permit
    (D) circumvent
    (E) concede

10. Shin-soo thought it was unfair that his teacher ------ him for turning in late assignments when the teacher was always tardy in grading papers.

    (A) indicted
    (B) glorified
    (C) promoted
    (D) replicated
    (E) disclosed

11. If sentence completion problems ------ you, try asking a teacher or tutor about methods that can help you understand them better.

    (A) refine
    (B) persuade
    (C) illuminate
    (D) interpret
    (E) perplex

12. The simple cake ------ nothing more than egg whites, sugar, and flour.

    (A) prohibits
    (B) forbids
    (C) consists of
    (D) excludes
    (E) obstructs

education
be smarter.

Unauthorized copying or reuse of any part of this page is illegal.

Version 1.3

Homework Passage 1 (Short)

Chances are that you have had the disease known as "the flu" at least once in your life. The flu, or *influenza* as it is more properly named, may seem like just a nuisance
Line to you. You may even get a flu shot every year to prevent
(5) coming down with the disease. But the flu is more than just a cause of fever, aches, and coughing; hundreds of thousands of people die from influenza each year, including thousands of Americans. In addition, new strains, such as the H1N1 virus, pose a greater threat,
(10) since most people lack the immune defenses to combat such unfamiliar diseases, and vaccines may not be created in time to inoculate those who are most vulnerable.

The flu was once an even greater menace, however.
(15) The worst flu outbreak, in 1918, resulted in millions of deaths in all parts of the world. It is estimated that as much as 5% of the world's population was killed in the 1918 outbreak. While modern medicine has reduced the deadliness of influenza greatly since 1918, it remains one
(20) of the world's costliest public health hazards.

13. As it is used in the passage, "pose" (line 9) most nearly means

   (A) pretend.
   (B) ask.
   (C) conceal.
   (D) present.
   (E) model.

14. The primary purpose of the passage is to

   (A) advocate for more efficient vaccine production.
   (B) outline the symptoms of an influenza infection.
   (C) show that a common illness is more dangerous than some may think.
   (D) praise the medical workers who have helped make influenza so much less deadly.
   (E) use first-person accounts to describe a historical event.

Homework Passage 2 (Short)

What is the oldest city or village in the United States? This is something of a trick question, since many cities predate the founding of the United States. But if
Line you guessed a European settlement like St. Augustine,
(5) Florida, you would be off by hundreds of years. While St. Augustine is the oldest European settlement, it was founded in 1565, more than 400 years after the village of Oraibi, a Native American village in what is now Arizona. Oraibi has been continuously populated by Hopi
(10) tribesfolk since at least 1150, and possibly longer. While Oraibi is a small, secluded village today, it once boasted a population in the thousands. The remaining Hopi tribesfolk still consider Oraibi to be a sacred place.

15. Which of the following statements best summarizes the main idea of the passage?

   (A) Several major cities, including Boston, New York, and Philadelphia, were founded well before 1776.
   (B) The oldest continuous settlement in the United States is a small Hopi village in Arizona.
   (C) Sacred villages are more likely to be preserved over long periods of time than other villages are.
   (D) St. Augustine, Florida, was founded by Spanish conquistadors in the 16th century.
   (E) The Hopi are one of the most important Native American tribes.

16. The passage states or implies that which of the following statements is true regarding Oraibi?

   (A) Its population is just a fraction of what it was hundreds of years ago.
   (B) It was established by early European colonists.
   (C) It no longer has any cultural significance.
   (D) It was founded more recently than St. Augustine.
   (E) It is now a suburb of a nearby, much larger town.

inoculate - vaccinate

imply: stronly suggest the truth or existence of (something not expressly stated.)

Unauthorized copying or reuse of any part of this page is illegal.

Homework Passage 3 (Short)

This passage is excerpted from the autobiography of the famed 19th- and 20th-century stage actress Sarah Bernhardt.

One day my mother took me on her knees and said to me, "You are a big girl now, and you must learn to read and write." I was then seven years old, and could
Line neither read, write, nor count, as I had been five years
(5) with the old nurse and two years ill. "You must go to school," continued my mother, playing with my curly hair, "like a big girl." I did not know what all this meant, and I asked what a school was.

"It's a place where there are many little girls,"
(10) replied my mother.

"Are they ill?" I asked.

"Oh no! They are quite well, as you are now, and they play together, and are very happy."

I jumped about in delight, and gave free vent to my
(15) joy, but on seeing tears in my mother's eyes I flung myself in her arms.

"But what about you, Mamma?" I asked. "You will be all alone, and you won't have any little girl."

She bent down to me and said: "God has told me that
(20) He will send me some flowers and a little baby."

17. One can infer from the passage that the narrator's educational development has thus far been

(A) outstanding.
(B) satisfactory.
(C) typical.
(D) deficient.
(E) ambitious.

18. The tone of the mother's comments to the narrator can best be described as

(A) indifferent.
(B) concerned.
(C) merry.
(D) harsh.
(E) reassuring.

Unauthorized copying or reuse of any part of this page is illegal.

Version 1.3

Homework Passage 4 (Long)

The following is an essay about the ways in which movies have portrayed space travel in the past 50 years.

Not all science fiction films are about space; nevertheless, space exploration and space travel have been common themes of many science fiction movies
Line over the decades. At times these forms of popular
(5) entertainment have attempted to depict space travel realistically but at other times they have completely ignored the laws of physics.

In 1968, Stanley Kubrick's *2001: A Space Odyssey* premiered. Kubrick wanted a movie that was
(10) based upon informed speculation about space travel more than three decades in the future, and he hired technical experts who could design realistic spacecraft. The movie featured a spaceplane, a giant wheeled space station, a lunar shuttle and even a "lunar bus" for transporting
(15) personnel over the moon's surface. But the primary spacecraft of the film was the 700-foot (213-meter)-long Discovery. The Discovery was nuclear-powered, but Kubrick made one major technical concession for storytelling's sake: he eliminated the giant radiators that
(20) would be necessary for such a craft because he thought his audience would wonder why a spacecraft had wings. The Discovery was also supposed to remind the audience of a human skeleton, with its large spherical command center, a long spine-like connecting boom, and its rocket
(25) engines at the other end.

Unlike many other films, *2001* also required its spacecraft to obey the laws of physics. Space is inconvenient for storytelling because the distances between all the interesting places are immense. Most
(30) writers get around this by inventing some magical propulsion technology, the "hyperdrive" in *Star Wars* or "jump points" in *Babylon 5*. On the other hand, *2001* had its spacecraft crawling between the planets at the glacial speed of 25,000 miles per hour (40,234 kilometers per
(35) hour), requiring large ships and special systems, like "sleep chambers" where personnel could hibernate like bears for months at a time.

By the 1970s and later, movie spacecraft tended to be super-sleek fightercraft, and often borrowed their
(40) design features from World War II aircraft. Darth Vader's TIE-fighter in *Star Wars*, for instance, had a control column influenced by the one used by the famed Royal Air Force Spitfire fighter of the Battle of Britain.

Most space-themed science fiction films tend to be
(45) focused on action and adventure. There have been a few notable exceptions, however. In addition to the aforementioned *2001*, Steven Spielberg's 1977 movie *Close Encounters of the Third Kind* attempted to capture the wonder of extraterrestrial contact. Instead of
(50) menacing aliens invading earth, the extraterrestrials in that movie were peaceful. Similarly, Jodie Foster's *Contact*, which premiered in 1997 and is based on a story by famed science author Carl Sagan, also took a more serious and joyful approach to the subject of
(55) humanity's first encounter with another civilization.

Filmmakers had generally shied away from realistic depictions of the actual Mercury, Gemini, and Apollo space missions. It was not until the 1990s that these got significant attention. In 1995, the movie *Apollo 13*, about
(60) the ill-fated mission that suffered an oxygen tank explosion on the way to the moon, was a smash hit. This inspired the HBO cable television network to create a series of one-hour films called *From the Earth to the Moon*, concerning different aspects of the space race. But
(65) by the beginning of the 21st century, zipping spaceships and bug-eyed monsters were once again in vogue. Science fiction film and television has returned to focusing on entertainment at the expense of accurately portraying space travel.

19. Which of the following would be the most fitting title and subtitle for the passage?

(A) Discovering the Discovery: The Making of Kubrick's *2001: A Space Odyssey*
(B) Science or Magic? Realism and Fantasy in Science-Fiction Novels
(C) Houston, We Have a Problem: Inaccuracies in Film Depictions of the Space Race
(D) The Future through the Years: A History of Space Travel in Film and Television
(E) Making *Contact*: The Life and Works of Legendary Author Carl Sagan

20. According to the passage, why is space "inconvenient for storytelling" (line 28)?

(A) The lack of gravity makes it difficult to plan standard action sequences.
(B) Characters must wear bulky spacesuits when leaving their ships.
(C) The large distances between key places make realistic space travel dull and time-consuming.
(D) The huge differences in temperature and pressure create major technical challenges in designing a spaceship.
(E) Writers' insufficient knowledge about other star systems forces them to focus on events near Earth.

21. According to the passage, in what respect does *2001: A Space Odyssey* differ from other film depictions of space travel?

    (A) In *2001*, spacecraft are limited to realistic speeds.
    (B) Many of the characters in *2001* are bug-eyed monsters.
    (C) The aliens in *2001* are evil and intent on conquering Earth.
    (D) *2001* features very unrealistic spacecraft.
    (E) The "hyperdrive" of *2001* allows its characters to travel quickly and easily to distance planets and stars.

22. In context, the word "glacial" (line 33) most nearly means

    (A) very slow
    (B) unfriendly
    (C) frigid
    (D) covered in ice
    (E) incredibly fast

23. The passage implies that all of the following are realistic spacecraft EXCEPT

    (A) a spaceplane that can take off from Earth and enter orbit
    (B) a lunar bus that travels along the moon's surface
    (C) a shuttle that travels between Earth and the moon
    (D) a wheel-shaped space station
    (E) a sleek, hyperdrive-powered fighting ship

24. Based on information in the passage, why might the makers of *Star Wars* have based their spacecraft on fighter planes?

    (A) A plane-like style of ship was necessary for the functioning of the film's "hyperdrive" systems.
    (B) They were more focused on the action and adventure of the story than on creating realistic spacecraft.
    (C) They wanted the ships to be reminiscent of human skeletons.
    (D) The design of World War II-era fighter planes was very similar to the design of modern spacecraft.
    (E) The ships in *Star Wars* needed to be able to fly through air as well as through space.

25. According to the passage, what caused the cable channel HBO to create a series of short films about the space race?

    (A) a desire to make more films with action and adventure
    (B) the writings of science author Carl Sagan
    (C) the great success of the film *Apollo 13*, which was also based on real events
    (D) the realistic space travel in Stanley Kubrick's *2001*
    (E) a sense that audiences wanted more evil aliens and fewer true-life tales

Unauthorized copying or reuse of any part of this page is illegal.

Version 1.3

Y4HW: Homework and Extra Practice

SC Topic: Using C2's 5-Step Method (Lesson Y2a) | **RC Topic:** Synthesizing (Lesson Y3b)

Homework Set 1

1. When she moved into her new office, Donna was surprised to find that her ------ had left behind an entire bucket full of assorted candies.

   (A) fanatic
   (B) antecedent
   (C) competitor
   (D) successor
   (E) traitor

   prefix: ante – Before or prior

2. The students who violated the new ------ to stop chewing gum in class were ------ to spend an afternoon cleaning hardened gum off of desks.

   (A) mandate . . compelled
   (B) veto . . discharged
   (C) distress . . conceded
   (D) decree . . forbidden
   (E) withdrawal . . obligated

3. Max was surprised to find that one of his neighbors was planning to ------ a perfectly good sofa, and offered to buy the sofa for five dollars.

   (A) acquire
   (B) compound
   (C) scrutinize
   (D) align
   (E) discard

4. Luisa ------ her grandfather not just because of his great wisdom, but also because of the ------, caring way he interacts with his family.

   (A) scorns . . devoted
   (B) salvages . . contrary
   (C) acclaims . . combative
   (D) venerates . . tender
   (E) indicts . . sympathetic

5. After spending almost a year in ------ on a remote island, Napoleon returned to France and formed a new government.

   (A) intimacy
   (B) goodwill
   (C) exile
   (D) alliance
   (E) modesty

6. Though the inhabitants of the neighborhood come from ------ backgrounds, they are united in their effort to make the neighborhood a better place.

   (A) duplicate
   (B) disparate
   (C) conventional
   (D) eccentric
   (E) equivalent

Post - after

disparate : various so different you can't compare
desperate : void of moral contraints in pursuit of goal

Mandate: order
compelled: forced labor

    Unauthorized copying or reuse of any part of this page is illegal.

Homework Set 2

7. Hal knew the history of American Presidents so well that he could ------ the names of all the Presidents, in order, in less than a minute.

    (A) omit
    (B) loiter
    (C) recite
    (D) disregard
    (E) hesitate

8. The tree disease proved to be quite ------, killing thousands of trees within a year of its discovery.

    (A) advantageous
    (B) benign
    (C) lofty
    (D) evocative
    (E) virulent

    virus

9. In an effort to ------ her father's stress, Indira brought him some headphones so that he could relax without hearing the ------ noises coming from outside.

    (A) agitate . . repulsive
    (B) alleviate . . raucous
    (C) pester . . blatant
    (D) soothe . . mild
    (E) attain . . muted

10. Holly's response seemed ------ to Richard, who thought that his question ------ a longer, more considerate answer.

    (A) blunt . . nullified
    (B) abrupt . . merited
    (C) civil . . deteriorated
    (D) verbose . . retracted
    (E) courteous . . warranted

11. Rather than answer the reporter's questions directly, the candidate ------ them and launched into a clearly rehearsed speech.

    (A) addressed
    (B) evaded
    (C) pondered
    (D) boasted about
    (E) enumerated

12. After serving her three-year term as mayor, Ms. Black ------ her former position as director of an architectural firm rather than run for re-election.

    (A) shunned
    (B) perceived
    (C) reverted to
    (D) repelled
    (E) persisted in

evocative:

benign :

evade:

raucous - obnoxious, loud

Unauthorized copying or reuse of any part of this page is illegal.

Version 1.3

Homework Passage 1 (Short)

The Japanese island of Yonaguni is famous for several things, including its native breed of small horse and a large population of hammerhead sharks that visit
Line its shores every winter. It also features the westernmost
(5) point in Japan, Cape Irizaki. Perhaps its most famous—and controversial—attraction, however, is the "Yonaguni Monument." This underwater rock formation consists of huge sandstone rocks, most with right angles, piled on top of each other in regular patterns. The largest rock is a
(10) sheet the size of five football fields and ninety feet tall. The Monument also features several pillars and a "road" that surrounds the base of the formation on three sides. There is even a star-shaped platform called "the Turtle."

While these spectacular features have led some to
(15) speculate the Monument was formed by humans thousands of years ago, the consensus of scientists is that it is an amazing but natural phenomenon caused by earthquakes and other geological activity.

Homework Passage 2 (Short)

Between the years of 1250 and 1500 A.D., the native islanders of Rapa Nui (what is now known as Easter Island) engaged in one of the most spectacular
Line enterprises of engineering and sculpture in human
(5) history. During this period, the Rapa Nui people carved nearly 900 gigantic stone statues with disproportionately large heads. Some of the figures, known as *moai*, were more than ten feet tall and weighed more than 150,000 pounds (about equal to 75 mid-size cars).

(10) Many of the *moai* were then transported large distances (several miles in some cases) and set upon elaborate stone platforms known as *ahu*. Archaeologists are still unsure of how this was accomplished. Some propose that the statues were "walked" by rocking them
(15) back and forth slowly across the ground. Others contend that the statues were rolled atop wooden logs. Both methods have flaws, however, and the true method may never be known.

---

13. Why does the author describe the Yonaguni Monument as being "controversial" (line 6)?

    (A) Several groups have claimed ownership of the part of the sea bed that includes the monument.
    (B) There is a dispute about whether the formation was created by natural forces or by humans.
    (C) Several people have been killed in shark attacks while diving in the vicinity of the monument.
    (D) Many scientists claim that the Yonaguni Monument does not exist.
    (E) The Japanese government has proposed destroying the rock formation in order to build an oil well.

14. Which of the following would make the most appropriate title for the passage?

    (A) Diving with Hammerhead Sharks
    (B) A "Monument" to the Power of Nature
    (C) The Power of Geometry
    (D) The Natural Wonders of Japan
    (E) The Ancient Civilization of Yonaguni

15. In context, the phrase "engaged in" (line 3) most nearly means

    (A) fought with
    (B) vowed to marry
    (C) caught the attention of
    (D) hired
    (E) carried out

16. The primary purpose of the passage was most likely to

    (A) criticize the Rapa Nui for wasting so much time carving and moving statues.
    (B) explain how large statues can be moved without modern technology.
    (C) contrast several cultures' sculptural traditions.
    (D) inform the reader about an impressive feat.
    (E) describe the culture of the native Easter Islanders.

Unauthorized copying or reuse of any part of this page is illegal.

Homework Passage 3 (Short)

No one knows the identities of the first people to have their photograph taken. In fact, it is unlikely that the subjects knew that they were being photographed; they
Line probably did not know that such a feat was possible.
(5)   The first photograph of a person was taken by Louis Daguerre in 1838, over a year before Daguerre's invention, which he modestly named the "daguerrotype," was announced and patented. The image, taken from a room high above a busy Paris intersection, shows streets
(10) and buildings, but only a few faintly visible people. In order to appear in the picture, a person would have had to remain still for nearly the entire period of the ten-minute exposure. The carriages and pedestrians on the street were thus not recorded.
(15)   Some people did remain motionless enough to appear, however. The most prominent is a man standing at a shoe-shine stall; the shoe-shine boy can also be seen, as can two figures seated at a café table nearby. Without knowing it, these anonymous figures made history,
(20) simply by remaining still at the right time.

17. According to the passage, why did the first people to be photographed probably "not know that such a feat was possible" (line 3)?

(A) Early photographic technology was known in other countries, but not in France.
(B) Before Daguerre, cameras could only take close-up images, and even those were blurry.
(C) The picture was taken before the first photographic technology was known to the public.
(D) All photographs at that time were taken of inanimate objects like trees and buildings.
(E) People at that time believed that living things should not be photographed.

18. Which of the following best summarizes the main idea of the passage?

(A) The daguerrotype was quickly surpassed by less complex technologies.
(B) Early photographs required a very long exposure time.
(C) The first people to be photographed probably did not intend to be in the picture.
(D) Photography did not become popular until Kodak invented the portable personal camera in 1902.
(E) Louis Daguerre chose to photograph empty intersections so that people would not obstruct his images.

Homework Passage 4 (Long)

The following is an excerpt from Oscar Wilde's classic novel The Picture of Dorian Gray, *first published in 1900. In the excerpt, an artist is showing his latest painting to his friend.*

In the centre of the room, clamped to an upright easel, stood the full-length portrait of a young man of extraordinary personal beauty, and in front of it, some
Line little distance away, was sitting the artist himself, Basil
(5) Hallward, whose sudden disappearance some years ago caused, at the time, such public excitement and gave rise to so many strange conjectures.
As the painter looked at the gracious and comely form he had so skillfully mirrored in his art, a smile of
(10) pleasure passed across his face, and seemed about to linger there. But he suddenly started up, and closing his eyes, placed his fingers upon the lids, as though he sought to imprison within his brain some curious dream from which he feared he might awake.
(15)   "It is your best work, Basil, the best thing you have ever done," said Lord Henry languidly. "You must certainly send it next year to the Grosvenor. The Academy is too large and too vulgar. Whenever I have gone there, there have been either so many people that I
(20) have not been able to see the pictures, which was dreadful, or so many pictures that I have not been able to see the people, which was worse. The Grosvenor is really the only place."
"I don't think I shall send it anywhere," he answered,
(25) tossing his head back in that odd way that used to make his friends laugh at him at Oxford. "No, I won't send it anywhere."
Lord Henry elevated his eyebrows and looked at him in amazement through the thin blue wreaths of smoke
(30) that curled up in such fanciful whorls from his cigarette. "Not send it anywhere? My dear fellow, why? Have you any reason? What odd chaps you painters are! You do anything in the world to gain a reputation. As soon as you have one, you seem to want to throw it away. It is
(35) silly of you, for there is only one thing in the world worse than being talked about, and that is not being talked about. A portrait like this would set you far above all the young men in England, and make the old men quite jealous, if old men are ever capable of any
(40) emotion."
"I know you will laugh at me," he replied, "but I really can't exhibit it. I have put too much of myself into it."

 Unauthorized copying or reuse of any part of this page is illegal.   Version 1.3

19. In context, the word "gracious" (line 8) most nearly means

    (A) elegant
    (B) generous
    (C) merciful
    (D) courteous
    (E) holy

20. Which of the following best describes Basil's reaction to his painting?

    (A) extreme dissatisfaction
    (B) delight bordering on disbelief
    (C) poorly hidden disappointment
    (D) obvious arrogance
    (E) dreadful confusion

21. Based on the third paragraph (lines 15-23), one can infer that Lord Henry's primary motivation in attending art galleries is

    (A) to learn about famous artists.
    (B) to admire the excellent art.
    (C) to relax in a quiet atmosphere.
    (D) to observe other people who seem to be interested in art.
    (E) to laugh at the artwork that he considers inferior.

22. Why does Lord Henry consider painters to be such "odd chaps" (line 32)?

    (A) They prefer the Academy to the Grosvenor.
    (B) They make other people jealous.
    (C) They disappear often, causing much excitement.
    (D) They put too much of themselves into their work.
    (E) They seem to lack a consistent drive for fame.

23. Based on evidence in the passage, which of the following phrases best describes the artist, Basil Hallward?

    (A) skillful but lazy
    (B) humorous and vulgar
    (C) silly and amateurish
    (D) fanciful and jealous
    (E) talented and unconventional

24. The primary purpose of the passage is to

    (A) describe the famous Grosvenor Art Gallery.
    (B) criticize Hallward for not displaying his painting.
    (C) contrast the reactions of two men to a fine work of art.
    (D) explain Lord Henry's high opinion of the Academy.
    (E) tell the life story of a renowned artist.

C2 education
be smarter.

SC TOPIC: Structure Words (Lesson Y5a)	RC TOPIC: Synthesizing (Lesson Y3b)

Homework Set 1

1. The constant chattering of the children in the theater ------ Marcellus' enjoyment of the movie.

    (A) augmented
    (B) concentrated
    (C) enhanced
    (D) detracted from
    (E) compiled

2. Unable to ------ the correct answer from any of the students, the teacher started giving hints and offering a reward to the first student to say the answer.

    (A) stifle
    (B) repress
    (C) elicit
    (D) deprive
    (E) confine

3. Though Nora was once quite ------ on stage, she quickly became ------ talking in front of the crowd, and within a few weeks she even began looking forward to it.

    (A) timid . . accustomed to
    (B) anxious . . uptight about
    (C) tranquil . . accommodated to
    (D) disinterested . . immature about
    (E) edgy . . vulnerable to

4. Although the wrestler was short, he was quite ------, and so his opponents often had difficulty throwing him down or knocking him over.

    (A) slender
    (B) sluggish
    (C) frail
    (D) lanky
    (E) stout

5. Raul's teacher was surprisingly ------ about ------ her deadline; she agreed to give him an extension without even asking him why he needed more time.

    (A) amenable . . deferring
    (B) reverting . . abridging
    (C) rigid . . compressing
    (D) submissive . . diminishing
    (E) unyielding . . prolonging

6. The artist was talented but ------, for her work was innovative and inspired, as she would never tire of bragging.

    (A) elegant
    (B) humble
    (C) conventional
    (D) sheepish
    (E) conceited

-4

Unauthorized copying or reuse of any part of this page is illegal.

Version 1.3

Homework Set 2

7. None of the children were allowed to go on the field trip unless their parents had given their ------ in writing.

   (A) prominence
   (B) discontent
   (C) indictment
   (D) condemnation
   (E) consent

8. Preeti told her supervisor that ten days was ------ amount of time to complete the project and asked for an additional five days to work on it.

   (A) an eccentric
   (B) an inadequate
   (C) a sufficient
   (D) an equivalent
   (E) a superfluous

9. The analyst ------ the increase in the unemployment rate to the ------ economy, which, he explained, had caused companies to cut back on their workforces.

   (A) attributed . . proceeding
   (B) restrained . . circumventing
   (C) ascribed . . deteriorating
   (D) perplexed . . declining
   (E) sacrificed . . alleviating

10. The issue was quite ------ when it was debated in the general assembly, with politicians on both sides ------ that the other side was immoral and irresponsible.

   (A) gratifying . . charging
   (B) mellow . . conceding
   (C) combative . . discounting
   (D) contentious . . alleging
   (E) congruous . . acclaiming

11. When the famous athlete was caught driving drunk, he was immediately and severely ------ by writers and fans alike, who accused him of setting a poor example for others.

   (A) evaded
   (B) venerated
   (C) infused
   (D) denounced
   (E) entrusted

12. The curved mirror was designed to ------ people's reflections so that even skinny people would appear to be fat.

   (A) echo
   (B) speculate
   (C) fret about
   (D) revert
   (E) distort

Unauthorized copying or reuse of any part of this page is illegal.

Homework Passage 1 (Short)

Earth's geography may seem to be static and unchanging; after all, even the fastest-moving land masses move only a few centimeters each year. Over a
Line long enough period of time, though, those centimeters
(5) start to add up to kilometers, and continents start to collide and separate.

Around 250 million years ago, the Earth looked very different. Rather than seven separate continents, there was just one. Geologists call this super-continent
(10) *Pangaea*, after the Greek words *pan* ("all") and *gaia* ("Earth"). The echoes of Pangaea can still be seen today in any map of the world: the eastern border of South America and the western border of Africa fit together like gigantic puzzle pieces.

13. Which of the following titles would be most appropriate for the passage?

   (A) All About the Metric System
   (B) The Unchanging Geology of Earth
   (C) Greek Words in Science
   (D) A Prehistoric Super-Continent
   (E) Slow and Steady Wins the Race

14. The passage implies that which of the following is true?

   (A) Earth's geography is fixed and will not change in the future.
   (B) Eastern South America was once connected to western Africa.
   (C) Mountains are formed by continental collisions.
   (D) Continents move quickly and unpredictably.
   (E) *Pangaea* was well known to ancient Greek geologists.

Homework Passage 2 (Short)

The most important American opera of the 20th century was not even recognized as an opera at first, although it is easy to understand why critics were
Line unprepared to fully appreciate such a groundbreaking
(5) work. When it debuted in 1935, *Porgy and Bess* was noteworthy for many reasons: it had an all-black cast during the height of the segregation era; its composer (George Gershwin) was known for "popular" music and had little experience with opera; and the music blended
(10) traditional opera with newer forms like blues and jazz.

While Gershwin considered *Porgy and Bess* to be his masterpiece, and fans flocked to see performances across the country, it would not be recognized as an opera until the 1970s. Since then, it has become a regular
(15) part of the repertoire of all major American opera houses. Its use of African-American actors and musical styles has also been highly influential in later 20th-century theater and opera.

15. According to the passage, when *Porgy and Bess* came out, most opera critics responded to it with

   (A) disrespect.
   (B) delight.
   (C) ambivalence.
   (D) awe.
   (E) nastiness.

16. The author of the passage would most likely agree that *Porgy and Bess* was

   (A) highly traditional.
   (B) ahead of its time.
   (C) interesting but ultimately forgettable.
   (D) unpopular with audiences and critics alike.
   (E) wrongly classified as an opera.

Unauthorized copying or reuse of any part of this page is illegal.

Version 1.3

Homework Passage 3 (Short)

Contrary to the way pirates are depicted in many modern films and novels, their lifestyle was not one of carefree sailing punctuated by frequent thrilling battles.
Line Furthermore, very few pirates were able to make much
(5) money or elude authorities for more than a few years. The typical pirate was a poor sailor who joined a pirate crew because of (usually false) promises of great riches and adventure. The pirate's life was extremely dangerous, not just due to battles with other ships, but
(10) also because of fierce storms and devastating illnesses brought about by poor diet and hygiene. Few pirates buried their treasure (indeed, few had enough treasure to merit a burial), and most either gave up the practice to become legal sailors in some country's navy, or died at
(15) sea at a young age. Even the notorious pirate Blackbeard was not able to acquire enough wealth or power to avoid the authorities: from his peak in 1717, his forces were gradually reduced until he was killed by the navy of Virginia colony in late 1718. He had been a pirate
(20) captain for only about two years.

17. Which of the following statements most accurately identifies the main idea of the passage?

   (A) Pirate treasure can be found buried on islands throughout the Caribbean Sea.
   (B) The life of a pirate was harsh and dangerous.
   (C) Pirates remain a threat to ships in certain parts of the world.
   (D) Movies often distort historical reality.
   (E) Blackbeard does not deserve his reputation as a fearsome pirate.

18. According to the passage, the average pirate's career was

   (A) thrilling.
   (B) profitable.
   (C) harmless.
   (D) carefree.
   (E) brief.

Homework Passage 4 (Long)

This passage is an overview of many different studies of gangs in the United States.

Gangs vary tremendously in composition and activities. Irving Spergel suggests the following working definition: "juveniles and young adults associating
Line together for serious, especially violent, criminal behavior
(5) with special concerns for 'turf.'" Turf can signify the control of a physical territory, a criminal enterprise, or both.

Defense of turf can lead to extreme violence. As Captain Raymond Gott of the Los Angeles Sheriff's
(10) Office says, simply "wearing the wrong color in a certain neighborhood can get you killed." Turf lines are normally drawn in the neighborhoods, but gang rivalries also have a devastating impact on schools. Often, even non-gang members begin bringing weapons to school for
(15) "protection" from robberies and gang violence.

Asian, black, Hispanic, white and interracial gangs exist, ranging in size from a few members to thousands. Ages range from preteen to adult, but the average age is dropping—from 15 in 1984, to 13½ today. The vast
(20) majority of gang members are male.

Most gang members advertise their membership by distinctive dress and behaviors, including handkerchiefs and shoelaces of specific colors, jewelry, tattoos, jargon, and hand gestures. They mark their territory and
(25) challenge other gangs with spray-painted graffiti or gang symbols.

According to Larry Rawles, deputy director of Philadelphia's Crisis Intervention Network, gang membership offers kids status, acceptance, and self-
(30) esteem they haven't found elsewhere. In poorer communities, a breakdown of family and community structures may leave kids more receptive to gang recruitment. However, gangs can also form in affluent areas among kids who feel alienated from friends and
(35) families.

Financial gain is a powerful motive for gang involvement, especially for impoverished youths with poor education and lack of access to decent jobs. The vast sums of money available through the drug trade
(40) have increased the size of gangs, both by recruitment and by longer retention of members. Despite this drug-related wealth, only a few adult gang members make large sums of money. Most low-level drug dealers receive so little compensation that they must also work a minimum-wage
(45) mainstream job in order to support themselves.

Aware that courts treat juveniles far more leniently than adults, gang leaders shield themselves by using juvenile gang members as everything from lookouts to gang hitmen. Drug trafficking makes traditional turf
(50) battles bloodier by providing the money for sophisticated weaponry, and it creates new sources of conflict as rival gangs fight over lucrative drug territories.

Unauthorized copying or reuse of any part of this page is illegal.

19. According to the passage, in what way has gang activity had "a devastating impact on schools" (line 13)?

   (A) Young gang members gain so much wealth that they feel no need to attend school.
   (B) Students in gangs get lower test scores.
   (C) Schools are often located on the boundary between the "turf" of two or more gangs.
   (D) Gang-specific clothing has forced many schools to institute dress codes.
   (E) Gang violence threatens the safety of every student, even non-gang members.

20. In the context of the passage, "advertise" (line 21) most nearly means

   (A) conceal
   (B) sell a product
   (C) publicly present
   (D) intimidate
   (E) pay for television commercials

21. A boy from a wealthy neighborhood is most likely to join a gang because he

   (A) enjoys the colors and hand gestures that the gang uses.
   (B) has high self-esteem and wants to take over the gang.
   (C) is getting poor grades in school.
   (D) feels isolated from his family and peers and wants to belong to a group.
   (E) knows that he can earn far more money as a low-level drug dealer than his parents earn.

22. How is the drug-related wealth of a gang most likely to be distributed, based on information in the sixth paragraph (lines 36-45)?

   (A) The young gang members who sell the drugs on the street keep most of the money.
   (B) The money is distributed equally among all gang members.
   (C) Half of the money is given to the low-level dealers and the other half is used to buy weapons and jewelry.
   (D) The adults who run the gang keep most of the money, giving only small amounts to the younger members.
   (E) Most of the money goes toward buying more property to expand the gang's "turf."

23. According to the passage, why do adult gang leaders rely on juvenile members for many illegal tasks?

   (A) If caught, the juvenile members are less likely to receive a severe penalty from the court system.
   (B) Most teenagers drop out of gangs after the graduate from high school.
   (C) Juvenile members are particularly eager to obtain large amounts of money.
   (D) Adolescents are less likely to be arrested or the victim of gang violence than older gang members are.
   (E) Young members are more skilled at most illegal activities than older members.

24. According to the passage, which of the following is NOT a characteristic of a gang?

   (A) It is predominantly male.
   (B) It engages in criminal activity.
   (C) It always exists in a poor community.
   (D) It uses specific colors, clothing, and language to distinguish itself from other gangs.
   (E) It is concerned with controlling "turf."

Unauthorized copying or reuse of any part of this page is illegal.   Version 1.3

Y6HW: Homework and Extra Practice

SC TOPIC: Structure Words (Lesson Y5a)	RC TOPIC: Finding Evidence (Lesson Y6b)

Homework Set 1

1. The party featured ------ decorations, expensive food, and a huge ice sculpture that must have cost a fortune.

   (A) deficient
   (B) moderate
   (C) commonplace
   (D) lavish
   (E) inferior

2. Whether he was politely declining an invitation or graciously accepting it, Jason was always ------.

   (A) eccentric
   (B) intrusive
   (C) cordial
   (D) savage
   (E) boisterous

3. Glenda, who strongly disliked most young-adult literature, thought that she would ------ the novel about the magic school, but she actually found it to be ------.

   (A) despise . . enchanting
   (B) denounce . . repulsive
   (C) adore . . engaging
   (D) retain . . mediocre
   (E) savor . . horrid

4. Vanya was sometimes ------ around strangers, but it was not ------ for her to be talkative and friendly, either.

   (A) bashful . . peculiar
   (B) blatant . . exotic
   (C) vulgar . . chronic
   (D) timid . . routine
   (E) rowdy . . anomalous

5. Faced with the unpleasant choice between two foods he hated, Mr. Nguyen decided to have the dish that he considered slightly less ------.

   (A) dreadful
   (B) tempting
   (C) luscious
   (D) savory
   (E) pliable

6. Troy did not sleep at all last night because of the ------ barking of the dog next door.

   (A) scarce
   (B) incessant
   (C) indistinct
   (D) incidental
   (E) benign

Unauthorized copying or reuse of any part of this page is illegal.
C2 education
be smarter.

Homework Set 2

7. In the official ceremony, the mayor ------ Ms. Lomax for her tireless work at the homeless shelter and her other ------ acts.

    (A) condemned . . philanthropic
    (B) acclaimed . . stern
    (C) ascribed . . vengeful
    (D) denounced . . jagged
    (E) commended . . benevolent

8. In order to ------ her parents into thinking that she was studying, Ursula hid her comic book within a textbook.

    (A) disclose
    (B) concede
    (C) attain
    (D) proclaim
    (E) deceive

9. The study found that an unhealthy diet can ------ a child's growth and that, conversely, a more ------ diet can accelerate growth.

    (A) inhibit . . wholesome
    (B) sustain . . perilous
    (C) obstruct . . deleterious
    (D) constrain . . wicked
    (E) collaborate . . healthful

10. Rather than continue doing all of her group's work, Eve decided to ------ a few of the tasks to the other members.

    (A) accumulate
    (B) shroud
    (C) delegate
    (D) withhold
    (E) evade

11. The lobby of the fancy new hotel is quite ------, as it is over fifty feet high and can hold over 2,000 people.

    (A) restless
    (B) expansive
    (C) minute
    (D) petite
    (E) confined

12. Because Ally is ------ airsickness, she takes an anti-nausea pill before every flight.

    (A) alleviated by
    (B) susceptible to
    (C) exempt from
    (D) immune to
    (E) ineligible for

Unauthorized copying or reuse of any part of this page is illegal.

Homework Passage 1 (Short)

Two of the most dangerous drugs in the world are produced from plants. Cocaine comes from the coca plant, while heroin is derived from the opium poppy
Line plant. Unlike coca, which is concentrated in South
(5) America, opium production occurs in three source regions—Southeast Asia, Southwest Asia, and Latin America—creating a worldwide problem. While an undetermined amount of the opium is consumed in the producing regions, a significant amount of the drug is
(10) converted to heroin and sent to the primary consuming markets—Europe and North America. The routes, volume, and methods for the shipment of heroin vary between the producing regions. Heroin from all three regions reaches the United States, using all forms of air,
(15) maritime, and overland conveyances. Higher purity levels and lower prices have fueled a rise in heroin use in the last 20 years.

13. According to the passage, a primary difference between cocaine and heroin is that heroin is

   (A) predominantly shipped by sea.
   (B) made from plants that grow in South America.
   (C) produced in more parts of the world.
   (D) generally less expensive.
   (E) used by many fewer people in the United States.

14. The primary purpose of the passage is most likely to

   (A) illustrate the damaging health effects of heroin use.
   (B) contrast two common illegal drugs.
   (C) describe how opium is turned into heroin.
   (D) inform the reader about a dangerous substance.
   (E) list the most profitable crops grown in Latin America.

Homework Passage 2 (Short)

In the year 1054, astronomers from around the world—including Koreans, Chinese, Native Americans, and Arabs—noticed a new light in the sky. It was bright
Line enough that it was clearly visible for more than three
(5) weeks, even during the day. This light was an example of what modern astronomers call a "supernova": an exploding star that releases an unfathomable amount of energy, all in a matter of weeks or months. The 1054 supernova expelled more energy than our sun will release
(10) in its entire lifetime.

The supernova of 1054 created a spectacular field of debris known as the Crab Nebula. The remnant of the star that went supernova is still in the center of the nebula; it is now a super-dense star called a "pulsar." The
(15) pulsar emits a flash (or "pulse") of energy toward Earth 30 times each second, and its density is equivalent to the entire human population of Earth compressed to fit inside a thimble.

15. The "new light in the sky" (line 3) was actually

   (A) an existing star that exploded.
   (B) a comet.
   (C) a planet.
   (D) an entirely new star.
   (E) a meteor entering Earth's atmosphere.

16. Which of the following titles would be most appropriate for the passage?

   (A) Astronomy Before the Telescope
   (B) What Is a Pulsar?
   (C) A "Super" Astronomical Event
   (D) The Life Cycle of the Sun
   (E) Major Events of the Eleventh Century

Homework Passage 3 (Short)

Generally speaking, the planes of today are far larger than their counterparts from the early days of commercial aviation. There is one extremely large (pun intended)
Line exception to this rule, however: the Hughes H-4 Hercules
(5) of the 1940s. The Hercules, which was developed by the American billionaire Howard Hughes, remains to this day the plane with the longest wingspan to ever successfully fly. To give an idea of the craft's immensity, its wings stretched over 320 feet from end to end—
(10) longer than a football field. It had eight 4,000 horsepower engines and weighed 400,000 pounds. It was infamous for both its impractical size and for being made of wood rather than metal; reporters mockingly dubbed it "The Spruce Goose."
(15) The Hercules only flew one time, on a test flight in 1947. Since then, it has been carefully preserved in various hangars and museums. More than 60 years later, it is now little more than a relic, even if no new plane has surpassed its size.

17. The passage implies that "reporters" (line 13) considered the H-4 Hercules to be

    (A) an intermediate step toward an even larger plane.
    (B) a remarkable achievement.
    (C) outdated and almost primitive.
    (D) interesting but too expensive.
    (E) ridiculous and bulky.

18. According to the passage, what is the primary legacy of the H-4 Hercules?

    (A) Many commercial aircraft today are made of wood like the Hercules.
    (B) It paved the way for even larger, heavier planes.
    (C) The H-4 design made its builder, Howard Hughes, extremely rich and famous.
    (D) Hundreds of H-4 planes were produced and used in military operations through the 1970s.
    (E) It still holds the record for the plane with the longest wingspan to actually fly.

Homework Passage 4 (Long)

This passage is a 2009 news article that outlines the possible benefits of a new robot designed to interact with astronauts.

NASA will launch the first human-like robot to space later this year to become a permanent resident of the International Space Station. Robonaut 2, or R2, was
Line developed jointly by NASA and General Motors under a
(5) cooperative agreement to develop a robotic assistant that can work alongside humans, whether they are astronauts in space or workers at GM manufacturing plants on Earth.

The 300-pound R2 consists of a head and a torso
(10) with two arms and two hands. R2 will launch on space shuttle Discovery as part of the STS-133 mission planned for September. Once aboard the station, engineers will monitor how the robot operates in weightlessness.

R2 will be confined to operations in the station's
(15) Destiny laboratory. However, future enhancements and modifications may allow it to move more freely around the station's interior or outside the complex.

"This project exemplifies the promise that a future generation of robots can have both in space and on Earth,
(20) not as replacements for humans but as companions that can carry out key supporting roles," said John Olson, director of NASA's Exploration Systems Integration Office at NASA Headquarters in Washington. "The combined potential of humans and robots is a perfect
(25) example of the sum equaling more than the parts. It will allow us to go farther and achieve more than we can probably even imagine today."

The dexterous robot not only looks like a human but also is designed to work like one. With human-like hands
(30) and arms, R2 is able to use the same tools station crew members use. In the future, the greatest benefits of humanoid robots in space may be as assistants or stand-ins for astronauts during spacewalks or for tasks too difficult or dangerous for humans. For now, R2 is still a
(35) prototype and does not have adequate protection needed to exist outside the space station in the extreme temperatures of space.

Testing the robot inside the station will provide an important intermediate environment. R2 will be tested in
(40) microgravity and subjected to the station's radiation and electromagnetic interference environments. The interior operations will provide performance data about how a robot may work side-by-side with astronauts. As development activities progress on the ground, station
(45) crews may be provided hardware and software to update R2 to enable it to do new tasks.

R2 is undergoing extensive testing in preparation for its flight. Vibration, vacuum and radiation testing along with other procedures being conducted on R2 also benefit
(50) the team at GM. The automaker plans to use technologies from R2 in future advanced vehicle safety systems and manufacturing plant applications.

"The extreme levels of testing R2 has undergone as it prepares to venture to the International Space Station
(55) are on par with the validation our vehicles and

Unauthorized copying or reuse of any part of this page is illegal.

components go through on the path to production," said Alan Taub, vice president of GM's global research and development. "The work done by GM and NASA engineers also will help us validate manufacturing (60) technologies that will improve the health and safety of our GM team members at our manufacturing plants throughout the world. Partnerships between organizations such as GM and NASA help ensure space exploration, road travel, and manufacturing can become even safer in (65) the future."

19. Which of the following would be the most fitting title for the passage?

(A) Safety Practices in GM Manufacturing Plants
(B) A History of Human-like Robots
(C) The International Space Station
(D) A Pioneering Robot
(E) The Cold Depths of Space

20. One can infer which of the following statements from the first sentence of the second paragraph (lines 9-10)?

(A) R2 is too heavy to operate on Earth.
(B) R2 has limited mobility because it does not have legs.
(C) GM will not benefit from the R2 project.
(D) Scientists are confident that R2 will work perfectly in the harsh environment of space.
(E) Astronauts will not find many uses for R2.

21. According to John Olson (line 21), what is the relationship between humans and robots?

(A) Robots can perform any task that a human can, and do it more safely.
(B) Humans and robots together can accomplish more than either group could accomplish on its own.
(C) Humans and robots would both be better off if they worked separately rather than as a team.
(D) Robots are much more likely to harm humans than to help them.
(E) Humans can only benefit a small amount from interacting with robots.

22. In the context of the passage, "intermediate" (line 39) most nearly means

(A) soothing
(B) transitional between different environments
(C) neither light nor heavy
(D) broadcast over the internet
(E) related to one who tries to end disputes

23. The passage states that engineering team is interested in how R2 responds to exposure to each of the following EXCEPT

(A) a vacuum
(B) electromagnetic interference
(C) harmful bacteria
(D) vibration
(E) radiation

24. Based on the quote in lines 53-65, what does Alan Taub consider to be the most important benefit of the R2 project?

(A) cheaper automobiles
(B) greater capacity for exploring distant worlds
(C) innovation that makes robots more common in everyday life
(D) the ability to completely replace humans on the International Space Station
(E) increased safety for humans

25. In what way does R2 differ from human astronauts, according to the passage?

(A) It will be limited to only one part of the space station.
(B) It is not shaped like a human in any way.
(C) It cannot use the same tools that humans use.
(D) It will perform supporting roles on the space station.
(E) It cannot be directly exposed to the extreme temperatures of space.

26. Which of the following best states the passage's main idea?

(A) Workers at GM auto plants are afraid that they could be replaced by a new, human-like robot.
(B) The R2 robot project could benefit both the space program and workers on Earth.
(C) R2 is still a prototype and cannot yet operate in the harsh conditions of space.
(D) Humans are inferior to robots like R2 that can easily perform many dangerous tasks.
(E) Robots are becoming increasingly human-like in appearance and function.

SC Topic: Meaning Words (Lesson Y7a)	RC Topic: Finding Evidence (Lesson Y6b)

Homework Set 1

1. The meeting began on a ------ note when Trey accused a co-worker of stealing his work, but all bitter feelings had been ------ by the meeting's end.

   (A) verbose . . delegated
   (B) cordial . . soothed
   (C) discordant . . alleviated
   (D) fond . . prolonged
   (E) contentious . . aggravated

2. Rather than ------ her printer's ink supplies by printing the 100-page document, Allison chose to read the document on her computer.

   (A) supplement
   (B) deplete
   (C) elicit
   (D) escalate
   (E) salvage

3. The doctors assured Harriet that the surgery would leave only a small, almost ------ scar, and that no one would notice it from far away.

   (A) expansive
   (B) evident
   (C) imperceptible
   (D) explicit
   (E) apparent

4. My grandmother's ------ television is so old that it does not even have a remote control; you have to get up to change the channel.

   (A) novel
   (B) dazzling
   (C) antiquated
   (D) contemporary
   (E) innovative

5. Myron was unable to ------ having a slice of cake; later, he would regret his ------ decision to violate his diet.

   (A) detract from . . considerate
   (B) circumvent . . tactful
   (C) delegate . . pliable
   (D) refrain from . . impulsive
   (E) conspire . . hasty

6. Thanks to some ------ maneuvering by its CEO, the company increased its profits and productivity in the last quarter.

   (A) lunatic
   (B) incoherent
   (C) repulsive
   (D) shrewd
   (E) eccentric

Unauthorized copying or reuse of any part of this page is illegal.

Homework Set 2

7. Before he retired, the chairman named his daughter as his ------ so as to keep the foundation in the family.

   (A) successor
   (B) precursor
   (C) foe
   (D) antecedent
   (E) immortal

8. Kira was ------ employee: she worked continuously for eight hours a day, or longer if required.

   (A) an apathetic
   (B) a tardy
   (C) an evocative
   (D) a sluggish
   (E) an industrious

9. Not even the constant rain could ------ the children's enthusiasm for miniature golfing; as they played, they laughed as much as ever.

   (A) enact
   (B) ascribe
   (C) pioneer
   (D) extinguish
   (E) institute

10. In addition to ------ the essay's excellent organization and well-supported thesis, Mr. Keating chose to criticize its ------ vocabulary and style.

    (A) retracting . . substandard
    (B) denouncing . . prominent
    (C) lauding . . inferior
    (D) indicting . . satisfactory
    (E) commending . . versatile

11. After his accident, the formerly sociable man became ------, rarely venturing out into public except when required.

    (A) reclusive
    (B) festive
    (C) accommodating
    (D) cultivated
    (E) carefree

12. The marathon runner was ------ in his determination to finish the race despite his cramping legs, and ------- to the end.

    (A) resolute . . persevered
    (B) incessant . . withdrew
    (C) flimsy . . sustained
    (D) wavering . . evaded
    (E) persistent . . terminated

Unauthorized copying or reuse of any part of this page is illegal.

C2 education
be smarter.

Homework Passage 1 (Short)

Three centuries ago, the English scientist Isaac Newton calculated, from his studies of planets and the force of gravity, that the average density of the Earth is
Line twice that of surface rocks and therefore that the Earth's
(5) interior must be composed of much denser material. Our knowledge of what's inside the Earth has improved immensely since Newton's time, but his estimate of the density remains essentially unchanged. Our current information comes from studies of the paths and
(10) characteristics of earthquake waves traveling through the Earth, as well as from laboratory experiments on surface minerals and rocks at high pressure and temperature.

13. According to the passage, the Earth's interior

  (A) has changed greatly since Newton's calculations.
  (B) is much denser than its surface.
  (C) remains completely unknown to scientists.
  (D) is very similar to its exterior.
  (E) is mostly hollow.

14. Which of the following best states the main idea of the passage?

  (A) Despite not having modern knowledge, Isaac Newton correctly estimated the Earth's density.
  (B) Unlike other planets, Earth has a dense core.
  (C) Geologists must rely upon centuries-old estimates about the Earth.
  (D) Studying earthquakes can tell us a lot about the composition of the Earth.
  (E) Scientific knowledge is constantly growing.

Homework Passage 2 (Short)

"Seek first to understand, then to be understood," recommends the psychologist Stephen Covey. He and many others believe this precept is paramount in
Line interpersonal relations, particularly for school officials.
(5) To interact effectively with anyone—teachers, students, community members, even family members—you need first to understand where the person is "coming from."

Next to physical survival, Covey observes, "the greatest need of a human being is psychological
(10) survival—to be understood, to be affirmed, to be validated, to be appreciated." When you listen carefully to another person, you give that person "psychological air." Once that vital need is met, you can then focus on influencing or problem-solving. The inverse is also true.
(15) School leaders who focus on communicating their own "rightness" become isolated and ineffectual.

15. Which of the following best summarizes the "precept" (line 3) described in the passage?

  (A) Most people do not care if they are understood as long as they are not insulted.
  (B) It is better to understand other peoples' viewpoints than to prove the superiority of your own viewpoint.
  (C) Psychological survival is even more important than physical survival.
  (D) Leaders should maintain a psychological distance from others.
  (E) Good listeners are well liked but unsuccessful because they spend less time advocating for their own ideas.

16. As it is used in the passage, the word "affirmed" (line 10) most nearly means

  (A) ignored.
  (B) insisted.
  (C) hardened.
  (D) announced.
  (E) acknowledged.

Unauthorized copying or reuse of any part of this page is illegal.   Version 1.3

Homework Passage 3 (Short)

So-called "quiz shows" have been a part of television since its beginnings. The format remains popular today with such long-running hits as *Jeopardy!*
Line and *Who Wants to Be a Millionaire?* During their heyday
(5) in the 1950s, however, quiz shows captured the public imagination to a degree rarely seen since.

The most-watched quiz show of this era was *Twenty-One*, which was loosely based on the card game of the same name (also known as blackjack). *Twenty-One* grew
(10) in popularity as a teacher named Herbert Stempel embarked on a long run as the show's champion. Stempel finally lost to the handsome college instructor Charles van Doren, who would prove to be even more popular.

Soon after his defeat, Stempel claimed that the show
(15) was rigged, and that he had been forced to allow van Doren to win. Though many dismissed Stempel's allegations, other contestants later came forward with similar stories. Van Doren eventually admitted that the show's producers had coached him on the correct
(20) answers. In the aftermath, *Twenty-One* was cancelled, and the quiz show genre lost much of its credibility.

17. The passage implies that most of today's quiz shows are

   (A) more difficult than those from earlier eras.
   (B) corrupt and untrustworthy.
   (C) largely ignored by the general public.
   (D) somewhat less popular than the shows from the 1950s.
   (E) derived from card games.

18. According to the passage, van Doren's success on *Twenty-One* was primarily due to

   (A) good fortune.
   (B) his extraordinary memory.
   (C) his handsomeness.
   (D) help from others.
   (E) his extensive education.

Unauthorized copying or reuse of any part of this page is illegal.

Homework Passage 4 (Long)

This passage describes some of the changes brought about in journalism by the invention of digital photography.

Digital technologies have greatly changed the working methods for photojournalists on assignment and brought major operational and economic advantages to
Line news organizations. In traditional photography,
(5) photographers could not be sure of what they had until they processed their film. Digital cameras have display screens that allow photojournalists to review what they have shot while still covering an event. They can decide whether they have the story-telling photographs or need
(10) to continue shooting. They can delete inadequate pictures and try them again. They can fill gaps in the visual narrative.

Two major changes serve both photojournalists and their news organizations. Considerable time is saved by
(15) eliminating the darkroom phase of traditional photography. Time formerly required to process film, make prints and send those prints through the engraving process can now be spent covering the event. By one photographer's account, at least 25 minutes are saved by
(20) eliminating chemical processing. Much time is also saved on the logistics of getting the images back to the publication. Instead of driving back to the office, photographers can plug the camera's memory cards into their laptop computers, select and caption the images,
(25) and transmit them by cell phone back to their publication's picture desk. This logistical advantage can work from the football stadium across town or from a news event in a foreign country. It is particularly advantageous when covering events close to deadline.
(30) Conversion to digital has brought many economic advantages to news organizations. Substantial savings result from converting from a wet-chemistry darkroom to a digital operation. They include the costs of film, photographic paper, and chemistry, which are no longer
(35) needed. A roll of film, for example, can only be used once, but a computer chip can be erased and reused continually. Another savings is the overhead cost of maintaining the darkroom itself that typically consumed sizeable space. There are savings from not having to
(40) dispose of dangerous chemicals, which is also a plus for the environment. Although considerable investment is required for digital cameras and the computer hardware, software, and storage space required for a digital photographic system, the conversion brings a net savings.
(45) Probably the greatest advantage to the organization is an operational one. Concurrent with the development of digital photography, newspapers and magazines transformed their printing process from the traditional system in which printers composed pages in a backshop
(50) to one where editors and designers produced pages on computers in the newsroom. This computerized pagination requires computer-compatible images. Many publications also have online editions, and digital photographs meld smoothly into the production of these
(55) websites. Online editions offer a major advantage to

photojournalists who can get more of their work published and have it available to the public for a longer time. Newsprint is expensive, and space for photographs is limited. There are no comparable limitations on
(60) displaying several images from a news event or an enterprise project on the web, and they can remain online as long as the publication chooses to archive them. Many newspapers, notably The Washington Post, have website branches that showcase the work of their
(65) photojournalists.

It seems safe to predict that the future of photojournalism will continue to follow technological developments in digital photography. While there may be a few scattered news operations that the revolution has
(70) not yet touched, the profession has undergone a technological transformation.

19. The primary purpose of the passage is to

  (A) outline some of the major benefits of the change from traditional to digital photography.
  (B) argue that news organizations should resist the urge to switch to digital photography.
  (C) chronicle the history of newspaper photography.
  (D) discuss the future of online journalism.
  (E) praise the Washington Post for its innovative approach to photojournalism.

20. What digital innovation has allowed photographers to "fill gaps in the visual narrative" (lines 11-12)?

  (A) The possibility of displaying many photographs online.
  (B) The large investment required to buy a digital camera.
  (C) The ability to view photographs while still at an event.
  (D) The invention of computerized pagination.
  (E) The light weight of digital cameras.

21. Which of the following time-consuming processes has been eliminated by digital photography?

  (A) Transmitting pictures to the newspaper office using a cell phone.
  (B) Producing a computerized version of a newspaper.
  (C) Erasing old photographs.
  (D) Developing photographs in a darkroom.
  (E) Placing photographs online.

Unauthorized copying or reuse of any part of this page is illegal.   Version 1.3

22. The passage implies that the greatest cost involved in digital photography is from

    (A) developing film.
    (B) disposing of chemicals.
    (C) buying new equipment.
    (D) traveling to foreign countries.
    (E) maintaining a darkroom.

23. Based on the fourth paragraph, one can infer that author considers the greatest advantage of digital publishing to be

    (A) a streamlined and efficient process for editing and printing.
    (B) the ability to produce an online edition.
    (C) the added space from not having to maintain a darkroom.
    (D) the ability to take hundreds of pictures at once.
    (E) a lack of dangerous chemicals.

24. Why are news organizations able to put more photographs in their online editions than in their print editions?

    (A) Many newspapers cannot print color photographs.
    (B) There are fewer space and cost limitations in the online edition.
    (C) Photographers would rather see their images online than in a newspaper.
    (D) Digital photographs are not compatible with print technology.
    (E) Photographers cannot submit photographs over their cell phones if they want the pictures to be in a newspaper.

25. Based on the last paragraph, which of the following developments is most likely in the future?

    (A) a new approach that combines the speed of chemical darkrooms and the affordability of digital cameras.
    (B) further savings in time and money brought about by improved technology.
    (C) a continued battle between the advocates of traditional and digital photography.
    (D) a reduction in the number of photographs available online.
    (E) a return to traditional, film-based photography.

26. Which of the following is NOT an advantage of digital photography over traditional photography?

    (A) Digital cameras allow photographers to take more pictures at an event.
    (B) Digital processing is much faster and easier than traditional processing.
    (C) Digital photographs are cheaper to produce and process than traditional photographs.
    (D) Digital photography requires no hazardous chemicals.
    (E) Digital cameras and the computer hardware required to use them are extremely cheap.

Unauthorized copying or reuse of any part of this page is illegal.

SC Topic: Meaning Words (Lesson Y7a)	**RC Topic**: Eliminating Answers (Lesson Y8b)

Homework Set 1

1. Despite the many warnings of the weather forecasters, the drought did not ------ the town's water supply; in fact, the drought's effects were nearly -------.

   (A) deplete . . inconsequential
   (B) diminish . . drastic
   (C) squander . . blatant
   (D) persevere . . negligible
   (E) congregate . . crucial

2. The warrior was known to try to intimidate his opponents by screaming ------ as he charged at them.

   (A) leniently
   (B) ferociously
   (C) inaudibly
   (D) contentedly
   (E) sympathetically

3. The general ------ his order when he realized that it would be disastrous to continue with the current plan.

   (A) reiterated
   (B) acclaimed
   (C) rescinded
   (D) delegated
   (E) venerated

4. Quentin's doctor warned him that the medicine might cause headaches or nausea, but, fortunately, Quentin did not experience any ------ effects.

   (A) benign
   (B) mild
   (C) meager
   (D) adverse
   (E) temperate

5. When she found out that she had gotten the lead role in the play, Iris was ------ and let out a joyous scream.

   (A) elated
   (B) apathetic
   (C) resentful
   (D) enraged
   (E) gloomy

6. In order to become a more ------ computer user, Jae ------ several classes at the local community college.

   (A) competent . . circumvented
   (B) ridiculous . . cherished
   (C) effectual . . invalidated
   (D) vulgar . . enlisted in
   (E) proficient . . enrolled in

Unauthorized copying or reuse of any part of this page is illegal.

Version 1.3

Homework Set 2

7. After he was caught driving 35 miles over the speed limit, Jasper's driver's license was ------ for a year and he was ------ to do 100 hours of community service.

   (A) ratified . . perplexed
   (B) retracted . . pardoned
   (C) accredited . . obligated
   (D) upheld . . lauded
   (E) revoked . . compelled

8. The ------ expression on the principal's face indicated that he did not believe a word of the boy's excuse.

   (A) absorbing
   (B) assured
   (C) incredulous
   (D) appreciative
   (E) gullible

9. Because she was ------ and able to give ------, simple explanations of complex concepts, Ms. Escalante was an excellent Calculus teacher.

   (A) conventional . . verbose
   (B) eloquent . . superfluous
   (C) reclusive . . compact
   (D) articulate . . concise
   (E) incoherent . . expansive

10. The company encouraged all of its employees to complete their assignments in a ------ manner by giving them bonuses for each assignment completed ahead of schedule.

    (A) prompt
    (B) deceased
    (C) inadvertent
    (D) delinquent
    (E) evocative

11. Although she usually enjoys just about any social activity, Brandy ------ karaoke because she considers her singing voice to be too high-pitched.

    (A) despises
    (B) commends
    (C) esteems
    (D) indulges in
    (E) savors

12. Kris preferred to deal with real-life problems such as how to dig a whole quickly rather than ------ ones like the meaning of life.

    (A) tangible
    (B) abstract
    (C) authentic
    (D) substantial
    (E) concrete

Homework Passage 1 (Short)

The practice of slavery dates back as far as recorded history (and likely much further); it was an accepted practice throughout nearly every major culture on every
Line inhabited continent. This widespread acceptance should
(5) not be taken to imply that no one fought against this horrific practice, however. Slave revolts followed slavery nearly everywhere, and abolitionism (the movement that aims to eliminate slavery in all its forms) is nearly as old as slavery itself.
(10) The first successful (recorded) attempt to eliminate slavery was by the Persian Emperor Cyrus the Great in the mid-6th century B.C.E. Over the next two thousand years, rulers in various countries (from China and India to France and Norway) also banned either slavery or the
(15) buying and selling of slaves. Unfortunately, nearly all of these reforms were reversed by later rulers, It was not until the 1500s that the tide began to turn permanently against slavery. By the late 1700s, this tide began to accelerate; countries like Russia, Japan, Portugal, and
(20) Scotland, as well as the U.S. states of Vermont, Pennsylvania, and Massachusetts, were all early adopters of abolition.

13. The primary purpose of the passage is most likely to

   (A) praise those rulers who banned the slave trade.
   (B) show that certain regions were too cruel or prejudiced to ban slavery.
   (C) provide a brief history of efforts to eliminate slavery.
   (D) defend slavery as a natural condition of human society.
   (E) argue that no one opposed slavery for thousands of years.

14. The author's attitude toward abolitionism can best be described as

   (A) indifferent.
   (B) doubtful.
   (C) harsh.
   (D) sympathetic.
   (E) mocking.

Homework Passage 2 (Short)

Exotic species are organisms transported by humans, wildlife, wind, and water into regions where they did not historically exist. For instance, the zebra mussel and
Line green crab have had serious ecological and
(5) socioeconomic impacts from the Great Lakes to the Gulf of Mexico, and from the Atlantic to the Pacific oceans—and in rivers and lakes in between. According to the Aquatic Nuisance Species (ANS) Task Force, Great Lakes water users spend tens of millions of dollars on
(10) zebra mussel control every year. As a result of such consequences, the National Sea Grant College Program and other organizations are very concerned with the increasing number of aquatic exotic species. The full economic and ecological impacts of each exotic species
(15) are continually under investigation.

15. Throughout the passage, the term "exotic" is used to mean

   (A) foreign.
   (B) rare.
   (C) colorful.
   (D) exciting.
   (E) native.

16. Which of the following most clearly states the main idea of the passage?

   (A) All exotic species are transported by human activity.
   (B) The Great Lakes feature hundreds of aquatic species.
   (C) Exotic species pose a serious and growing ecological threat.
   (D) The green crab is the most damaging exotic species in the United States.
   (E) The zebra mussel is native to the Great Lakes.

Unauthorized copying or reuse of any part of this page is illegal.

Version 1.3

Homework Passage 3 (Short)

The first English-language crossword puzzle appeared in the *New York World* newspaper in 1913. The so-called "Word-Cross Puzzle" was written by Arthur *Line* Wynne, and while it lacked many features that we have
(5) come to associate with crosswords (such as square grids), it did have crisscrossing numbered clues that went both across and down. Within a few years, the puzzle's name had changed to "crossword," and its format had evolved into more or less the modern version. Soon thereafter, the
(10) crossword became hugely popular, spreading to hundreds of American newspapers. At first, it was dismissed as a fad, and even criticized for being "a primitive form of mental exercise." The crossword, however, was here to stay. Today, millions of people do crosswords every day,
(15) and the puzzles are published in dozens of languages. Some crossword constructors, like Will Shortz of the *New York Times*, have even acquired a sort of folk hero status among the aficionados of the genre.

17. According to the passage, some early critics of the crossword considered it to be

(A) too easy to solve.
(B) lacking in sophistication.
(C) openly discriminatory against women.
(D) unpopular.
(E) inaccessible to non-English speakers.

18. Which of the following titles would be most appropriate for the passage?

(A) A Primitive Hobby
(B) The Rise of the Crossword
(C) Fads of the Early 20th Century
(D) Crosswords In Foreign Languages
(E) Will Shortz: Puzzle Master

Unauthorized copying or reuse of any part of this page is illegal.

Homework Passage 4 (Long)

The following passage was written by a woman who, through the United States Peace Corps, helped farmers in the Dominican Republic improve their agricultural practices.

When I arrived in my community as the promised agroforestry technician and Peace Corps Volunteer, a number of men said to me, "I thought we were getting a
Line man."
(5)   I usually smiled and replied, "There must have been some sort of horrible mistake." They would smile back, and I would swallow hard, knowing my work was more than cut out for me. Living in a remote village in the mountains was difficult, but getting the male farmers to
(10) look to a female technician for help with their land seemed impossible.

For the first few months, a male technician working for a local nongovernmental organization took me under his wing. I accompanied him to the farmers' properties
(15) and began to get to know a few of the farmers this way. After some time mostly observing their work, I began to ask my own questions and make my own suggestions. I found the technician less responsive to me than the farmers were. I knew that I would have to make my
(20) break from the technician soon, or the locals would never listen to me. I took advantage of the days when the technician did not come up the mountain to work with the farmers one on one.

I would help the farmers with their work, talking
(25) about projects and possibilities for their land. I asked many questions and learned much more with the farmers than when I was with the technician. Nevertheless, in the first six months, I got very little accomplished with the men. In the meantime, I started a
(30) home-garden workshop for the women, to strengthen the existing gardens. We had weekly meetings and demonstrations, and each week worked in a different garden.

After spending months on the gardens, I tried once
(35) again to turn my attention to the farmers. Some days I would find myself alone, planting a hundred trees, and some days, with a group of farmers, planting 2,000 trees. I continued to wake up early every morning and strap on my work boots. After nine months working in my site, I
(40) had established a few strong friendships with farmers. I encouraged them to start building soil barriers in the dry season, in preparation for the next rains. Then, one morning, a farmer came to my house and asked me if I would like to come out to his land to start building
(45) barriers. I looked into his face, expecting him to laugh, but he was serious. In that moment, I felt nine months of persistence and struggle all come together.

After I worked a few weeks with that farmer, some of the other farmers came to me asking to build barriers
(50) as well. With three farmers and other helpers, we formed a work party and rotated our work among the different pieces of land. In two months, we had established more than 11,000 feet of barriers and I had created a strong bond with these men, who now talk with me daily about
(55) work and projects.

As a woman who works with male farmers all day long, while their wives stay close to home cooking, washing clothes, and tending to children, I am challenged
(60) every day. The work in the fields is often physically demanding, but with sheer persistence, I have managed to convince most of the farmers in my community that my work is useful. Although it took time to wedge myself into the farmers' lives, I feel I have accomplished
(65) something great. Today, I spend most of my time with the farmers. Recently, they even voted and made me the official "educator" of their farmers' association.

19. Which of the following would be the best title for the passage?

(A) Life in the Dominican Republic
(B) Farming in the 19th Century
(C) Learning to Teach the Farmers
(D) Innovative Farming Methods
(E) A Relaxing Trip to the Country

20. What is the most likely reason that the narrator says, "There must have been some sort of horrible mistake" (lines 5-6)?

(A) She wants to make fun of the farmers for being wrong.
(B) She is trying to explain how the mistake happened.
(C) She is responding to a difficult situation with humor.
(D) The Peace Corps had meant to send a man.
(E) She is worried that she is in the wrong community.

21. Why did the narrator's task seem "impossible" (line 11)?

(A) She doubted that she would survive the difficult conditions in the remote mountain region.
(B) Crops would not grow in the village's poor soil.
(C) She would not be able to win over the farmer's wives.
(D) She doubted that the male farmers would ever fully accept her and her ideas.
(E) Her fellow technician refused to show her around the village.

Unauthorized copying or reuse of any part of this page is illegal.

Version 1.3

22. Why did the narrator feel the need to separate herself from the male technician?

(A) The local farmers would not listen to her if she did not convince them that she had her own ideas.
(B) The male technician rarely talked to the farmers.
(C) She wanted to see areas of the village that he was not familiar with.
(D) The farmers refused to listen to a man.
(E) The technician was far more capable than she was.

23. What was the narrator's main accomplishment during her first six months on her own?

(A) She planted 100 trees a day by herself.
(B) She was named "educator" of the farmer's association.
(C) She was completely accepted by the men of the village.
(D) She helped a farmer build barriers around his farmland.
(E) She began a home-garden workshop for the farmers' wives.

24. What event proved to be a breakthrough in the narrator's relationship with the male farmers?

(A) when she planted 100 trees on her own
(B) when she toured the community with the male technician
(C) when one of the farmers asked her to help him build earthen barriers on his farm
(D) when she joked with them about the fact that they were expecting her to be a man
(E) when she helped the women with their gardens

25. Which of the following most nearly matches the meaning of the word "wedge" (line 63) as it is used in context?

(A) incline
(B) hold in place
(C) block from doing
(D) slice into small pieces
(E) force one's way into

26. Which of the following did the narrator NOT accomplish during her time in the farming community?

(A) planting thousands of trees
(B) building extensive earthen barriers
(C) educating the male technician about how to communicate with the farmers
(D) gaining the respect of the male farmers
(E) being appointed "educator" of the community

27. Which of the following best sums up the most important lesson that the narrator learned in the Dominican Republic?

(A) Men will never accept women's opinions on farming.
(B) When meeting with a group of strangers, it is important to speak to the people of your gender first.
(C) Gender discrimination is widespread in Larin America.
(D) Helping those in other countries is a horrible mistake.
(E) With good ideas, hard work, and persistence, you can accomplish tasks that seem to be impossible.

Unauthorized copying or reuse of any part of this page is illegal.

Y9HW: Homework and Extra Practice

SC TOPIC: Predicting Answers (Lesson Y9a)	RC TOPIC: Eliminating Answers (Lesson Y8b)

Homework Set 1

1. The magician was so skillful that he could ------ even those people who doubted that magic even existed.

   (A) retract
   (B) fatigue
   (C) attain
   (D) afflict
   (E) astonish

2. Greg was utterly ------ after his team's humbling defeat, but he managed to graciously congratulate the other team for playing well.

   (A) elated
   (B) optimistic
   (C) dejected
   (D) ecstatic
   (E) content

3. Luigi was unable to ------ interest in the movie after the first few minutes; it was so boring that he took a nap instead.

   (A) revoke
   (B) deplete
   (C) sustain
   (D) subside
   (E) venerate

4. Ebenezer showed his great ------ for the poor by dismissing their pleas for charity with an angry grunt.

   (A) prominence
   (B) regard
   (C) sentiment
   (D) disdain
   (E) mandate

5. Though rats are supposedly ------ sight in New York City, Zelda found them to be quite ------; she could not get more than a brief glimpse of them.

   (A) an anomalous . . evasive
   (B) a commonplace . . straightforward
   (C) an extraordinary . . cordial
   (D) a customary . . elusive
   (E) an eccentric . . outspoken

6. When his neighbors found out that Vladimir had been spreading ------ rumors, they unanimously ------ him for his hurtful lies.

   (A) concise . . indicted
   (B) malicious . . denounced
   (C) negligible . . commended
   (D) benign . . condemned
   (E) adverse . . adored

Unauthorized copying or reuse of any part of this page is illegal.

Version 1.3

Homework Set 2

7. The city of New Orleans was nearly destroyed by Hurricane Katrina, but its citizens showed great ------ by helping the city to rebuild.

    (A) resignation
    (B) delicacy
    (C) resilience
    (D) passiveness
    (E) descent

8. In an effort to ------ her team on to victory, Candace started singing the school fight song and high-fiving her teammates.

    (A) dampen
    (B) spur
    (C) dismay
    (D) prohibit
    (E) concede

9. Occasionally, Geoff will ------ a hamburger, but these urges are always ------ and before long, he goes back to being his normal, vegetarian self.

    (A) yearn for . . persistent
    (B) scoff at . . momentary
    (C) long for . . incessant
    (D) crave . . transitory
    (E) despise . . concise

10. Although none of the friends had more than two dollars, they were able to ------ their money to buy a large pizza.

    (A) aggregate
    (B) sever
    (C) disperse
    (D) squander
    (E) isolate

11. The ------ between the two friends was so painful that not even a heartfelt apology could ------ it.

    (A) rift . . alleviate
    (B) bond . . counteract
    (C) discord . . dissect
    (D) juncture . . moderate
    (E) coalition . . alienate

12. Several teenagers were ------ the amusement park today for trying to cut in line to one of the rides; they will not be allowed back in the park for a week.

    (A) enchanted by
    (B) warranted in
    (C) expelled from
    (D) enticed to
    (E) lauded by

Homework Passage 1 (Short)

Some commonly accepted stories about early America are not supported by much actual historical evidence. Contemporary accounts indicate that the first
Line Thanksgiving was very little like the event
(5) commemorated in today's school pageants. George Washington never chopped down a cherry tree (and never confessed to doing so, either). Benjamin Franklin never flew a kite in a lightning storm with only a small key standing between him and electrocution.

(10) Of course, these stories do have some slight basis in fact. The Pilgrims no doubt had good reason to be thankful for the Native Americans' help, as they likely would not have survived without the aid of friendly tribes. Even his enemies regarded Washington as being
(15) scrupulously honest. Franklin did perform many pioneering experiments with electricity, including one in which he flew a kite into a storm cloud to charge a primitive battery, although this version of the experiment was much safer and did not involve a key or an actual
(20) lightning strike.

13. The primary purpose of this passage is to

   (A) convince the reader to study early American history.
   (B) praise Benjamin Franklin for risking his life in the name of science.
   (C) criticize Native Americans for treating the Pilgrims poorly.
   (D) argue that all stories about the Founding Fathers are myths with no basis in fact.
   (E) correct some common misconceptions about American history.

14. One can infer from information in the passage that the author considers the "commonly accepted stories about early America" (lines 1-2) to be

   (A) more fiction than fact.
   (B) verified by the historical record.
   (C) more interesting than stories about recent historical figures.
   (D) utterly without factual basis.
   (E) originally authored by Benjamin Franklin.

Homework Passage 2 (Short)

Public art is not a new phenomenon. Publicly displayed statues of important figures date back at least to ancient times; one could also make the argument that
Line monumental constructions such as the pyramids of Egypt
(5) and Stonehenge constitute public art. The purpose of public art, however, has changed in recent years. Whereas statues and monuments are mainly intended to memorialize a person or event, many new projects are abstract sculptures that use shapes and reflections to
(10) create a unique sense of space.

Perhaps the best example of this type of modern public art is the *Cloud Gate*, a huge sculpture by Anish Kapoor located in Chicago's Millennium Park. Nicknamed "the Bean" for its distinctive shape, this
(15) mirror-polished steel structure is 66 feet long and 42 feet tall, weighing over 100 tons. It has quickly become the most popular spot in Chicago for tourists to take pictures, as it allows for uniquely distorted views of the city as well as the people in and around the sculpture.

15. The first paragraph of the passages (lines 1-10) are primarily intended to

   (A) describe an example of a large-scale abstract sculpture.
   (B) identify the greatest public art projects in the world.
   (C) compare the sizes and shapes of various monuments.
   (D) draw a contrast between a traditional art form and its modern equivalent.
   (E) claim that all new public art projects are abstract sculptures.

16. According to the passage, the *Cloud Gate* is a popular place "to take pictures" (line 17) mainly because it

   (A) offers a unique perspective of a city.
   (B) memorializes a great disaster.
   (C) is larger than Stonehenge.
   (D) serves as a monument to a beloved former leader.
   (E) is located near an acclaimed restaurant.

Unauthorized copying or reuse of any part of this page is illegal.

Version 1.3

Homework Passage 3 (Short)

The worst natural disaster in the history of the United States (at least in terms of loss of life) was the Galveston Hurricane of 1900. At the time, weather
Line forecasting methods were primitive, and the residents of
(5) Galveston (a city and island off the coast of Texas) had little warning that a storm was headed their way. As a result, very few people in the path of the hurricane were prepared for the 20-foot storm surge that flooded the entire island (for reference, the highest hill on the island
(10) at the time was only 9 feet above sea level). Most people who could not take refuge in a tall building were drowned, and many others were killed by fierce lightning and debris flung through the air by the 135 mile-per-hour winds. Over 8,000 people lost their lives, and nearly all
(15) the buildings on the island were destroyed or heavily damaged.

To protect against future disasters, the citizens of Galveston responded by building a seawall and raising the entire island by 15 to 17 feet, an astonishing feat of
(20) engineering that has likely saved hundreds of lives during subsequent storms.

17. The primary purpose of the passage is to

(A) list the deadliest hurricanes in history.
(B) illustrate the geography of Galveston in 1900.
(C) describe the consequences of a famous natural disaster.
(D) identify the most spectacular act of engineering of the 20th century.
(E) explain how a hurricane is formed and gathers strength.

18. According to information in the second paragraph (lines 17-21), Galveston is now

(A) just as vulnerable to deadly storm surges.
(B) mostly abandoned due to damage from the 1900 hurricane.
(C) the largest city in Texas.
(D) far more prepared to handle a severe hurricane.
(E) ignorant of its past

Homework Passage 4 (Long)

The following excerpt describes how the language and culture of the Tlingit people (a Native American tribe from southeastern Alaska) changed during the 20th century.

I grew up as a young Tlingit boy during the 1930s. In my earliest memories, I can recall my grandmother holding me on one of her knees and singing her clan
Line songs to me in Tlingit. Very early she taught me the
(5) dance movements of a male dancer. As she held me she would tell me that I would soon be too big for her to hold on her lap. During the summers, I was expected to help my grandmother pick berries and make noise to chase away any bear that might be in the berry patch. Later,
(10) when I learned to row a double-ended rowboat, it was my job to transport her across the inlet to the smokehouse several times a day to tend the fire used for smoking the sockeye salmon that I had helped harvest with my Tlingit uncle.
(15) The rest of the time I was free to play with my friends in the community—rowing around the bay, swimming in the creek, and playing in the woods and under the family sawmill. We played in the fish cannery where we built huge caves out of empty boxes that would
(20) be used after our parents and other members of the community finished harvesting.

I spoke English but I remember the villagers of my grandparents' generation speaking to each other in Tlingit. When my parents and uncles spoke to each other
(25) they used English. When they spoke to the older generation they spoke Tlingit. I attended celebrations where the elders stood and talked in Tlingit. Dancers, wearing Tlingit costumes, danced to the music of clan songs and chanted in tune and time to a Tlingit drum.
(30) During my middle childhood years I spent much of my time with my uncles. They taught me the skills to hunt for deer, trap mink, make fishing nets, jig for halibut, use nets to catch the early spring steelhead and sockeye salmon, and make and blow an instrument used
(35) for calling deer. Much of our food was from the wild or from my grandmother's garden. During the winter, I watched the totem pole carvers in Klawock working on the large totems for the park that was being built.

Throughout their lives my uncles continued to speak
(40) to each other in Tlingit and to non-Tlingit speakers in English. I listened but not enough to really learn it. I understood it when I was younger and around my grandmother, for she spoke only Tlingit to her sons and to me. But I spoke to her in English. In this way I was
(45) like most of my generation in Klawock, who did not learn the Tlingit language. We spoke to our parents, aunts, and uncles in English, building a new language base for the government schools we attended.

The language base of my children and grandchildren
(50) is English. These two younger generations seldom, if ever, hear Tlingit spoken because they live in other parts of the country, seldom coming to Alaska where—to this day—they might hear my uncles and their generation speak the language to one another. I have lost the

Unauthorized copying or reuse of any part of this page is illegal.

(55) language, my children never learned the language, and my grandchildren have lost the opportunity to learn the language.

19. Which of the following best describes the state of the Tlingit culture during the 1930's?

    (A) It had become completely Americanized.
    (B) While the children tried to keep the traditional practices alive, the adults mostly spoke English.
    (C) Everyone in the tribe spoke both English and Tlingit equally well.
    (D) Its traditions were still alive, though more in the older generations than with the children.
    (E) The Tlingit language was still the only one used in the village.

20. The narrator's childhood can best be described as one that was

    (A) completely carefree.
    (B) ruined by several tragic events.
    (C) filled with both work and play.
    (D) lonely and boring.
    (E) wholly devoted to hard work.

21. During the narrator's early childhood, in which of the following scenarios would the speaker be most likely to use the Tlingit language?

    (A) when an old woman is speaking to her husband
    (B) when a middle-aged man is speaking to his brother
    (C) when a middle-aged woman is speaking to her daughter
    (D) when a young boy is speaking to his father
    (E) when a young girl is speaking to her grandmother

22. According to the passage, the narrator's uncles taught him many skills, most of which were focused on

    (A) how to find and prepare food in the wild.
    (B) dancing in the Tlingit ceremonies.
    (C) how to properly speak the Tlingit language.
    (D) how to operate the family sawmill and cannery.
    (E) singing the clan songs.

23. In what way was the author "like most of [his] generation" (line 45)?

    (A) He helped to carve the clan totem poles.
    (B) He had no respect for his elders.
    (C) He danced in the Tlingit ceremonies.
    (D) He spoke Tlingit to his parents and grandparents.
    (E) He had only a limited understanding of the Tlingit language and could not speak it.

24. According to the passage, which generation was able to speak both English and Tlingit fluently?

    (A) the narrator's grandparents' generation
    (B) the narrator's parents' generation
    (C) the narrator's generation
    (D) the narrator's children's generation
    (E) the narrator's grandchildren's generation

25. The primary purpose of the passage is to

    (A) criticize the younger generations for not learning the Tlingit language.
    (B) describe the traditional diet of the Tlingit people.
    (C) memorialize the language and traditions of a tribe that is slowly losing its cultural identity.
    (D) teach the reader how to hunt and fish.
    (E) contrast the Tlingit language and English.

Unauthorized copying or reuse of any part of this page is illegal.

Version 1.3

Y10HW: Homework and Extra Practice

SC Topic: Predicting Answers (Lesson Y9a)	RC Topic: Detail Questions (Lesson Y10b)

Homework Set 1

1. Hiro's friends ------ him to help them chose which movie to watch, but he was completely ------ and would not offer an opinion either way.

   (A) attained . . compassionate
   (B) revoked . . apathetic
   (C) appealed to . . subjective
   (D) implored . . indifferent
   (E) pleaded with . . absorbed

2. With ------ wave of her hand, Winifred dismissed her classmates, forgetting that this was not her mansion and they were not her servants.

   (A) a meek
   (B) a hesitant
   (C) an affectionate
   (D) a pompous
   (E) a cordial

3. The suspect's explanation seemed ------ to the detective, and indeed the suspect would eventually admit that he was not telling the whole truth.

   (A) credible
   (B) commendable
   (C) dubious
   (D) authentic
   (E) expansive

4. The old skating rink was now ------, but it had once been a popular place for young people to ------.

   (A) deserted . . rupture
   (B) animated . . aggregate
   (C) bustling . . migrate
   (D) vacant . . withdraw
   (E) desolate . . assemble

5. Unwilling to ------ the dispute between the two strangers, Alejandro chose to try to ignore their loud argument.

   (A) intervene in
   (B) elicit
   (C) shun
   (D) circumvent
   (E) elude

6. Though Lina's mother was strict, her father was much more ------, and even let her watch television until well past her bedtime.

   (A) negligible
   (B) stingy
   (C) reclusive
   (D) stern
   (E) indulgent

Unauthorized copying or reuse of any part of this page is illegal.
C2 education be smarter.

Homework Set 2

7. In less than 50 years, Chicago grew from a minor, not very wealthy city into one of the most ------ and influential cities in America.

   (A) repulsive
   (B) elusive
   (C) conventional
   (D) humble
   (E) prosperous

8. Catherine could not finish the project at the airport, for the noise of the terminal ------ her concentration and was not at all ------ to productivity.

   (A) deteriorated . . adverse
   (B) detracted from . . conducive
   (C) augmented . . contrary
   (D) escalated . . advantageous
   (E) diminished . . perplexing

9. After ------ search of every part of the mountain, the rescuers finally found the missing hikers, who were cold and hungry but otherwise fine.

   (A) an insufficient
   (B) a concise
   (C) a transitory
   (D) an exhaustive
   (E) a meager

10. After embarrassing herself by tripping on her way onto the stage, Shriya ------ some of her pride by performing a flawless ballet dance.

   (A) salvaged
   (B) devastated
   (C) despised
   (D) withered
   (E) depleted

11. Since he hated long car rides but enjoyed spending time with his friends, it was only natural that Colin would feel ------ about their upcoming road trip.

   (A) superfluous
   (B) invigorated
   (C) ambivalent
   (D) dejected
   (E) malicious

12. Although Hyun-hwan was too ------ to sing in front of strangers, he was a ------ singer and invariably impressed those who heard him.

   (A) discordant . . competent
   (B) agitated . . frail
   (C) cozy . . inept
   (D) elated . . deft
   (E) timid . . proficient

Homework Passage 1 (Short)

There are more people alive today in and around New York City than were alive in the entire world 10,000 years ago. New York City and its surrounding
Line areas boast roughly 20 million inhabitants, which ranks
(5) New York as the fourth-to-sixth largest city in the world, depending on who does the counting. By way of comparison, most estimates agree that there were only around five to ten million people alive in the year 8,000 B.C.E. (about 10,000 years ago).

(10) The world's population has risen quickly in the intervening time. It reached 50 million around 3,000 years ago, then 200 million by 1 A.D. (around 2,000 years ago). It reached 500 million sometime in the 1500s A.D. and topped one billion around 1800 A.D. In recent
(15) decades, the world has added a billion people every 12-15 years to reach its current level between 6 and 7 billion.

Experts disagree about the future of the world population. Some predict that it will peak at around 8
(20) billion in 2050; others foresee continued growth to 10 billion people—and beyond.

13. The passage states that New York City

(A) has many more people than all of Earth did in 8,000 B.C.E.
(B) is equivalent in population to the entire Earth in 1 A.D.
(C) is the largest city in the world today.
(D) will someday have more than 50 million residents.
(E) is declining in population.

14. Based on information in the passage, one can conclude that the world's human population

(A) is currently on the decline.
(B) will remain roughly constant until 2050.
(C) has experienced both rapid growth and abrupt declines in the past 1,000 years.
(D) has risen steadily throughout history.
(E) will certainly exceed ten billion in the near future.

Homework Passage 2 (Short)

Many of the most mysterious creatures on Earth reside in the depths of the ocean. While some of these are legitimately frightening, others simply have frightening
Line names. An example from this latter group is the vampire
(5) squid, a six-to-twelve-inch, eight-legged cephalopod that is related to both the regular squid and the octopus. The vampire squid gets its name not from any blood-sucking ability but rather from its deep red coloring. Its most interesting features are its tentacles, each of which glows
(10) with a soft blue light known as bioluminescence. The vampire squid, like other cephalopods, ejects ink when threatened, but its ink contains a special surprise: numerous soft blue lights like the ones on the tips of its tentacles. This display is meant to dazzle predators so as
(15) to allow the vampire squid to escape. The vampire squid also has the remarkable ability to "breathe" normally at depths of two to three thousand feet, despite the very low oxygen levels there. Only a handful of other creatures are able to live full-time at those depths.

15. The vampire squid can "dazzle predators" (line 14) by

(A) glowing blood red.
(B) sucking their blood with its tentacles.
(C) ejecting ink that contains glowing lights.
(D) using a toxin that stuns nearby creatures.
(E) breathing normally at great depths.

16. The author's attitude toward the vampire squid can best be described as

(A) affectionate.
(B) fascinated.
(C) disgusted.
(D) anxious.
(E) uninterested.

Homework Passage 3 (Short)

This passage is taken from a short story about a Chinese-American family coping with cultural changes.

My daughters are almost grown: sixteen and twelve. Mei-ling, the elder, makes her own cup of coffee, and twists her hair into a careless rope at the breakfast table;
Line Mei-po, tall and slender as a rice shoot, carries a
(5) backpack that weighs thirty pounds, as if at any moment she could be summoned to climb Mount Everest. They move through the apartment beginning at dawn: I open my eyes to the sound of the shower running, bare heels knocking along the hallway, a burst of music, a door
(10) slammed shut. When I walk into the kitchen, their eyes slide from the table to the floor to the television without looking up. *Zao*, I say, "Morning," and they stiffen, as if I've dropped a glass, or scraped my nails against a chalkboard. Sometimes I imagine I've stumbled into an
(15) opera at the pause between the overture and the aria, and at any moment their voices will twine together in lament. "Our father keeps us captive in his castle," I can hear them sing. "Rescue us!"

17. Based on information in the passage, which of the following statements is most likely to be true?

(A) The narrator's daughters are studying to be opera singers.
(B) Mei-ling is happy to be living with her mother.
(C) The narrator wakes up later than her daughters.
(D) The narrator's family is friendly and talkative.
(E) Mei-po enjoys mountain climbing.

18. The daughters' reaction to the narrator's greeting (line 12) can best be described as

(A) irritated.
(B) lively.
(C) tender.
(D) saddened.
(E) welcoming.

Homework Passage 4 (Long)

This passage, written in 1998, is an analysis of the ways in which children's literature treats girls differently than boys.

Gender bias exists in the content, language and illustrations of a large number of children's books. This bias may be seen in the extent to which a gender is
Line represented as the main character in children's books and
(5) how that gender is depicted.

Numerous studies analyzing children's literature find the majority of books dominated by male figures. For example, Ernst did an analysis of titles of children's books and found male names represented nearly twice as
(10) often as female names. She also found that even books with female or gender-neutral names in their titles in fact, frequently revolve around a male character. Many classics and popular stories in which girls are portrayed usually reflect stereotypes of masculine and feminine
(15) roles. Such gender stereotypes are prevalent not only in mainstream children's books but also in Newbery and Caldecott medal winners.

Children's books frequently portray girls as acted upon rather than active. Girls are represented as sweet,
(20) naive, conforming, and dependent, while boys are typically described as strong, adventurous, independent, and capable. Boys tend to have roles as fighters, adventurers and rescuers, while girls in their passive role tend to be caretakers, mothers, princesses in need of
(25) rescuing, and characters that support the male figure. Often, girl characters achieve their goals because others help them, whereas boys do so because they demonstrate ingenuity and/or perseverance. If females are initially represented as active and assertive, they are often
(30) portrayed in a passive light toward the end of the story. Girl characters who retain their active qualities are clearly the exception. Thus, studies indicate that not only are girls portrayed less often than boys in children's books, but both genders are frequently presented in
(35) stereotypical terms as well.

Many researchers and authors argue that readers identify with characters of their own gender in books. Therefore, the relative lack of girl characters in texts can limit the opportunity for girls to identify with their
(40) gender and to validate their place in society.

The manner in which genders are represented in children's literature impacts children's attitudes and perceptions of gender-appropriate behavior in society. Sexism in literature can be so insidious that it quietly
(45) conditions boys and girls to accept the way they 'see and read the world,' thus reinforcing gender images. This reinforcement predisposes children to not question existing social relationships. At the same time, however, books containing images that conflict with gender
(50) stereotypes provide children the opportunity to re-examine their gender beliefs and assumptions. Thus, texts can provide children with alternative role models and inspire them to adopt more egalitarian gender attitudes.
(55) Gender stereotypical roles are constraining to both

Unauthorized copying or reuse of any part of this page is illegal.

genders. Just as girls are trapped in passive and whiny roles, boys and men are rarely described as people demonstrating emotions of sadness and fear, having hobbies/occupations that are not stereotypically male and
(60) in roles in which they aren't competing or meeting high expectations. These stereotypes limit boys' and girls' freedom to express themselves and pressure them to behave in ways that are 'gender appropriate' rather than ways best suited to their personality.

19. The primary purpose of the passage is to

(A) reveal racial stereotypes in elementary-school textbooks.
(B) describe a troubling trend in children's literature.
(C) praise children's books for portraying boys as capable, brave, and persistent.
(D) define a difficult term using stereotypes.
(E) analyze gender bias in the works of J.K. Rowling.

20. According to the passage, children's books with female names in the titles

(A) often focus more on male characters than female ones.
(B) do not exist.
(C) are more common than books with male names in the titles.
(D) rarely rely on gender stereotypes.
(E) are unlikely to be illustrated.

21. The passage implies that award-winning children's books

(A) are more often based on female characters than other books.
(B) are just as likely as other books to contain stereotypical characters.
(C) teach young boys to be passive and naïve.
(D) are far more egalitarian than mainstream books.
(E) are completely without literary merit.

22. As it is used in the passage, the word "active" (line 19) most nearly means

(A) physically fit
(B) not dormant or extinct
(C) requiring a lot of energy
(D) acting independently
(E) frequently moving

23. According to the passage, how do female characters in children's books typically achieve their goals?

(A) by using their ingenuity to come up with a novel solution
(B) through the help of another person, usually a boy
(C) through good fortune
(D) by persevering through difficult events
(E) by winning an intensely fought competition

24. According to statements made in the fourth paragraph (lines 36-40), what is one of the main effects of the lack of female characters in children's books?

(A) Girls may experience lower test scores in reading.
(B) Boys may think that girls are the superior gender.
(C) Many children's books may sell fewer copies.
(D) Young girls may experience difficulty in identifying female role models in the books that they read.
(E) Some children may re-examine their assumptions about gender.

25. How do most children's books affect the way children "see and read the world" (lines 45-46)?

(A) They encourage children to find role models from the opposite gender.
(B) They convince girls to be more active and ambitious.
(C) They reinforce standard gender roles and encourage children to have stereotypical views of the world.
(D) They inspire children and adults alike to treat each gender equally.
(E) They ensure that boys will see themselves as weak and whiny.

26. The author of the passage would most likely argue that the stereotype of boys as competitive and fearless

(A) is troubling, but not representative of a larger problem.
(B) is harmful to both boys and girls.
(C) has little impact on the minds of young children.
(D) benefits young boys but constrains young girls who hope to be more independent.
(E) is extremely helpful to young boys with low self-esteem.

Y11HW: Homework and Extra Practice

SC TOPIC: Eliminating Answers (Lesson Y11a)	RC TOPIC: Detail Questions (Lesson Y10b)

Homework Set 1

1. Always ------ fellow, Englebert became even more friendly when there was free food available.

    (A) a dejected
    (B) a discordant
    (C) an innovative
    (D) an amiable
    (E) a contentious

2. The students were upset when the principal ------ that they wear uniforms, but because the school board had approved the order, the students had no choice but to ------.

    (A) pronounced . . evade
    (B) revoked . . persist
    (C) voided . . concede
    (D) confronted . . acclaim
    (E) mandated . . comply

3. The ------ composer was greeted with cheers, autograph requests, and other gestures of respect from the numerous admirers of his work.

    (A) perplexing
    (B) despicable
    (C) verbose
    (D) desolate
    (E) venerable

4. The novel's ------ plot was criticized by some for being complex and hard to follow.

    (A) pliable
    (B) straightforward
    (C) concise
    (D) intricate
    (E) transparent

5. Although Yadier felt no ------ toward Sheila, he could not ------ his laughter when she dropped her ice cream cone; he made it up to her by buying her a new one.

    (A) tenderness . . fortify
    (B) charity . . stifle
    (C) hostility . . enliven
    (D) sympathy . . stir
    (E) malice . . suppress

6. The actor's performance in the play was ------ failure; he forgot his lines repeatedly, spoke too softly to be heard, and even fell off the stage at one point.

    (A) an utter
    (B) an elusive
    (C) a transitory
    (D) a laudable
    (E) a negligible

Homework Set 2

7. In order to ------ more responses from his class, Mr. Weatherby promised to give two pieces of candy to anyone who could give a correct answer.

   (A) elicit
   (B) denounce
   (C) cloak
   (D) deplete
   (E) retract

8. As a child, Inez ------ to be an astronaut, but her parents were ------ that a little girl who was afraid of heights could ever fly into space.

   (A) yearned . . genuine
   (B) resented . . cordial
   (C) aspired . . dubious
   (D) alleviated . . assured
   (E) procrastinated . . skeptical

9. The museum's main ------, who donated five million dollars last year alone, is a famous local businesswoman.

   (A) recluse
   (B) benefactor
   (C) detractor
   (D) adversary
   (E) antecedent

10. Before he could properly ------ the value of the rare baseball card, the expert had to carefully examine its condition.

    (A) circumvent
    (B) scorn
    (C) appraise
    (D) offset
    (E) delegate

11. The artist's work has met with both ------- praise and harsh ------; critics seem to either love it or hate it.

    (A) indifferent . . indictment
    (B) effusive . . condemnation
    (C) expansive . . acclaim
    (D) ambivalent . . eccentricity
    (E) raucous . . proficiency

12. After eating only a small muffin for breakfast and missing lunch entirely, Carla was feeling quite ------.

    (A) saturated
    (B) resilient
    (C) incredulous
    (D) voracious
    (E) plentiful

Homework Passage 1 (Short)

From birth to death, our lives follow a complicated recipe of nature and nurture. While heredity affects our personality and health, how we live—our environment—
Line plays a huge role as well. Nonetheless, identifying
(5) genetic traits that influence our actions may help us learn how to manage unhealthy behaviors. One way that researchers are studying genes and behavior is by using model organisms that have similar genes and biochemistry to people. Recently, behavioral geneticists
(10) used fruit flies to look for genes that might be linked to aggression.

The researchers bred groups of flies separately for 28 generations, choosing the most aggressive males in the "high" group and the least aggressive males in the
(15) "low" group to start each new generation. Since the behavior of the two groups hardly differed at the end of the experiment, the researchers deduced that only a small component (about 10 percent) of the variation in aggression could be attributed to variation in genes.

Homework Passage 2 (Short)

In the year following the Japanese Empire's attack on the Pearl Harbor naval base in Hawaii on December 7, 1941, anti-Japanese hysteria began to flourish in all areas
Line of America, but in particular on the west coast. At the
(5) time, many Americans thought that a Japanese invasion of the west coast was imminent, though there is no evidence that the Imperial forces ever seriously considered such a bold attack. These irrational fears led military authorities, with the support of President
(10) Franklin Roosevelt, to remove many Japanese immigrants and American citizens of Japanese descent to internment camps in the center of the country.

Over 120,000 Japanese-Americans (two-thirds of them American citizens) were eventually relocated to
(15) these camps, and most were forced to remain for the duration of the war. The detainees were not compensated for their lost property, and the conditions at many of the camps were very poor.

In 1988, the United States government finally issued
(20) a formal apology, as well as monetary reparations of $1.6 billion, to the victims and their heirs.

13. The primary purpose of the passage is to

(A) describe the life cycle of the fruit fly.
(B) discuss the interaction between genes and behavior.
(C) critique a recent scientific study.
(D) prove that heredity is more influential than environment.
(E) compare human genetics to those of fruit flies.

14. The main conclusion of the research using "fruit flies" (line 10) is that

(A) humans and fruit flies have exactly the same genes and biochemistry.
(B) aggressiveness has no basis in the genes of fruit flies.
(C) male flies are far less aggressive than female flies.
(D) genes are relatively unimportant in determining a fly's aggressiveness.
(E) the lab environment reduces the frequency of flies' aggressive behaviors.

15. The author of the passage most likely considers the internment of Japanese Americans to be

(A) ultimately inconsequential.
(B) regrettable but necessary.
(C) beneficial but inadequate.
(D) illogical and unjust.
(E) completely justified.

16. The "detainees" (line 16) were relocated to internment camps primarily because they

(A) protested against the war.
(B) were of a particular ethnicity.
(C) chose to leave the west coast.
(D) were not American citizens.
(E) actively helped America's enemies.

Unauthorized copying or reuse of any part of this page is illegal.   Version 1.3

Homework Passage 3 (Short)

The forerunners of modern superheroes date back at least to early-20th-century fictional characters such as Zorro, Tarzan, and Popeye, all of whom had distinctive
Line abilities and fought enemies. One could argue, in fact,
(5) that centuries-old characters such as Hercules (from *The Iliad* and other mythology), Gilgamesh, and Robin Hood constitute superheroes. One quality that all of these characters (as well as the earliest comic-book superheroes from the 1930s) share is that they are
(10) uniformly male.

The first female superheroes did not appear until the early 1940s, but all of these were short-lived, secondary characters. The first influential superheroine, Wonder Woman, debuted in 1942. Despite Wonder Woman's
(15) long-lasting success, a trend of sexism in comic books continued for decades afterward. Most new female heroes were merely less-powerful versions of a male hero, nearly always with the immature suffix "girl" tacked onto their names (e.g., Spider-Girl, Batgirl, and
(20) Supergirl). Not until the late 1970s did superheroines begin to operate on a somewhat equal basis with their male counterparts.

17. The primary purpose of the passage is most likely to

    (A) provide a chronology of female superheroes.
    (B) compare mythical heroes to modern comic book heroes.
    (C) identify the most interesting superhero of the 20th century.
    (D) condemn the lack of gender equality in comic books.
    (E) propose a re-evaluation of late-1930s comic book superheroes.

18. According to the passage, what set Wonder Woman apart from earlier female superheroes?

    (A) She was merely a female version of "Wonder Man."
    (B) She had more powerful abilities.
    (C) She had a sidekick.
    (D) She was modeled on a character from a thousand-year-old fable.
    (E) She was a much more enduring character.

Homework Passage 4 (Long)

The following passage describes the contents of the United States Declaration of Independence and the circumstances in which it was written.

During June and July of 1776, the main question facing the Second Continental Congress at Philadelphia revolved around independence: Should the American
Line colonies represented at this Congress declare their
(5) separation and freedom from the United Kingdom of Great Britain? After intense debate, the delegates voted on July 2, 1776 in favor of Richard Henry Lee's resolution for independence. On July 4, the Congress discussed and approved, with a few changes, the formal
(10) Declaration of Independence written by Thomas Jefferson on behalf of a five-person committee appointed by Congress.

During July and August 1776, the Declaration of Independence was printed and distributed throughout the
(15) newly proclaimed United States of America. Americans recognized immediately that this document expressed widely held ideas about the proper purposes of government and the rights of individuals. George Mason expressed the same ideas about government and rights in
(20) similar words in Articles I-III of the Virginia Declaration of Rights, which was drafted and approved a few weeks before the Declaration of Independence. Many years later Jefferson acknowledged that the Declaration of Independence was "intended to be an expression of the
(25) American mind" and not an original or innovative statement.

The Declaration of Independence can be divided into four main parts. The first part is an introduction that states the purpose of the document, which was to explain
(30) why the American people were declaring independence from the government of Great Britain.

The second part is a theory of good government and individual rights generally accepted by Americans from the 1770s until today. In this theory, all individuals are
(35) equal in their possession of certain immutable rights. These rights are not granted by the government. Rather, they are inherent to human nature. Therefore, the first purpose of a good government is to secure or protect these rights. Further, a good government is based on the
(40) consent of the governed—the people—who are the sole source of the government's authority. If their government persistently violates this theory of good government, then the people have the right to overthrow it.

The third part of the document is a list of grievances
(45) against King George III, who was singled out to represent the actions of the British government. These grievances are examples of actions that violated the criteria for good government stated in the second part of the Declaration of Independence. These grievances,
(50) therefore, justify separation from the King's bad government and establishment of a good government to replace it.

The fourth and final part of the document is an unqualified assertion of sovereignty by the United States

(55) of America. It proclaims the determination of Americans to defend and maintain their independence and rights.

19. As it is used in line 21, what is the meaning of the word "drafted"?

   (A) called into service
   (B) drank
   (C) blown through the air
   (D) written
   (E) poured

20. Based on information in the passage, one can conclude that Thomas Jefferson had what opinion about the Declaration?

   (A) that it was a worthless, clichéd work
   (B) that George Mason used it as the basis for his Virginia Declaration of Rights
   (C) that it was highly innovative
   (D) that it had very little impact on the course of history
   (E) that it was an unoriginal but uniquely American document

21. According to the passage, the Declaration states that all individuals are equal because

   (A) they are born with the same human rights.
   (B) they are all equally intelligent and capable.
   (C) the government grants them the same rights.
   (D) the Magna Carta guaranteed equal treatment to all British citizens.
   (E) they have all been equally wronged by the actions of King George III.

22. What was the purpose of the third part of the Declaration?

   (A) to outline some generally accepted principles of good government
   (B) to state the Americans' determination to defend their rights
   (C) to state the purpose of the document
   (D) to ask whether the United States should declare themselves independent of Great Britain
   (E) to criticize King George III for his excesses and violations of Americans' rights

23. Which portion of the Declaration outlined the basic human rights at the center of the new nation's government?

   (A) none of them
   (B) the first part
   (C) the second part
   (D) the third part
   (E) the fourth part

24. The primary purpose of this passage is to

   (A) outline the major historical events of 1776.
   (B) argue that the Declaration of Independence was plagiarized.
   (C) criticize King George III for violating the principles of good government.
   (D) describe the significance of an important document.
   (E) analyze the writings of Thomas Jefferson.

Unauthorized copying or reuse of any part of this page is illegal.

Version 1.3

Y12HW: Homework and Extra Practice

SC Topic: Eliminating Answers (Lesson Y11a) | **RC Topic**: Word-in-Context Questions (Lesson Y12b)

Homework Set 1

1. The ------ writer managed to write over 100 pages about the ordinary events of his evening.

   (A) succinct
   (B) depleted
   (C) verbose
   (D) voracious
   (E) blunt

2. A congressperson should not be ------, and should stand up for his or her beliefs even if it means ------ his or her own party.

   (A) emphatic . . despising
   (B) timid . . dissenting from
   (C) insistent . . contradicting
   (D) vacillating . . conceding to
   (E) cowardly . . yielding to

3. In order to ------ the anxious children, the babysitter offered each of them a cookie.

   (A) placate
   (B) ridicule
   (C) agitate
   (D) scold
   (E) repel

4. After years of bitter conflict, the two nations experienced a ------ and entered into a more ------ relationship.

   (A) pact . . contentious
   (B) conventionality . . repulsive
   (C) reconciliation . . amiable
   (D) dubiousness . . cordial
   (E) rivalry . . engaging

5. When the journalist heard that she had won the Pulitzer Prize, she was ------, and began shouting joyously.

   (A) dejected
   (B) intricate
   (C) ecstatic
   (D) ambivalent
   (E) mournful

6. The only thing that ------ today's otherwise perfect weather was the huge amount of allergy-causing pollen in the air.

   (A) aggregated
   (B) venerated
   (C) purified
   (D) augmented
   (E) detracted from

Homework Set 2

7. A few abandoned and crumbling pyramids are the only ------ of the once-great city at Machu Picchu.

   (A) remnants
   (B) delegates
   (C) myths
   (D) comprehensions
   (E) vacancies

8. Lola's ------ lateness could be ------ her frequent and lengthy fits of daydreaming.

   (A) transitory . . attributed to
   (B) persistent . . alleviated by
   (C) recurrent . . repulsive to
   (D) perpetual . . ascribed to
   (E) hypothetical . . proficient with

9. Feeling that his old microwave was ------ now that he had a newer and more powerful model, Reginald donated the older microwave to charity.

   (A) requisite
   (B) momentous
   (C) inevitable
   (D) resolute
   (E) superfluous

10. The higher court ------ the law, saying that it did not violate the Constitution and thus could not be revoked.

    (A) suppressed
    (B) upheld
    (C) denounced
    (D) eluded
    (E) abolished

11. Dr. Andrews knew that the vaccine had a very high rate of effectiveness, but he was not ------ the precise figure.

    (A) complying with
    (B) evocative of
    (C) oblivious to
    (D) cognizant of
    (E) perplexed by

12. Elle was ------ worker, but she could not study at home because the noise there was not ------ to her concentration.

    (A) a diligent . . conducive
    (B) an expansive . . discordant
    (C) an indifferent . . effusive
    (D) a negligent . . advantageous
    (E) a studious . . adverse

Unauthorized copying or reuse of any part of this page is illegal.

Version 1.3

Homework Passage 1 (Short)

When someone asks us where we are from or what we do, most of us mention the town or city where we live, our occupation, where we attended school, or our
Line family heritage. We respond in terms of human
(5) communities, cultures, and geopolitical boundaries. We seldom, if ever, describe ourselves in terms of our ecological status in the natural world. We humans have so completely ordered, designed, and defined our physical environs and social milieu that our ecological
(10) connections have slipped from consciousness. Perhaps this is why we seem so unaware of our impact on nature and our rapid destruction of natural systems. We simply do not perceive ourselves as being part of the natural order of beings, even as our existence continues to
(15) depend in large part on resources provided by nature.

13. According to the author, why have "our ecological connections … slipped from consciousness" (lines 9-10)?

(A) Modern humans have no measurable impact on natural systems.
(B) Humans attempt to control and define as much of the world as possible.
(C) Most humans think of nature as the enemy of humanity.
(D) The world is now controlled by countries like the U.S. and China, which have poor education systems.
(E) Humans are no longer reliant on any part of the natural world.

14. As it is used in line 14, "order" most nearly means

(A) organized group.
(B) tidiness.
(C) peaceful state.
(D) sale.
(E) command.

Homework Passage 2 (Short)

Until its dissolution in the 1990s, Yugoslavia was a country of about 23 million people located in southeastern Europe, across the Adriatic Sea from Italy.
Line More than 15 ethnic groups lived in the former
(5) Yugoslavia. The bulk of the population, however, belonged to one of six related Slavic groups: Serbs, Croats, Slovenes, Bosnian Muslims, Macedonians, and Montenegrins. The Croats, Serbs, Muslims, and Montenegrins speak a common language, referred to as
(10) "Serbo-Croatian." But religious and other cultural differences, which have resulted from separate historical experiences, have divided these Slavic groups.

From the Middle Ages to 1918, most of these people lived in one of two empires, which dominated this part of
(15) Europe: the Hapsburg Empire, ruled from Vienna, and the Ottoman Empire, ruled by the Turks from Istanbul. The Slovenes and Croats lived under Hapsburg rule, while the Bosnians and most Serbs lived under Turkish authority. Serbia and Montenegro, though, had small
(20) independent kingdoms by the turn of the 20th century.

15. As it is used in line 5, "bulk" most nearly means

(A) awkwardness.
(B) majority.
(C) muscle.
(D) volume.
(E) obesity.

16. The people of Yugoslavia before 1918 can best be described as

(A) predominantly Slavic Muslims.
(B) independently governed.
(C) varied and divided.
(D) culturally and ethnically uniform.
(E) historically part of the same empire.

Homework Passage 3 (Short)

Half dance and half martial art, the Brazilian art form of *capoeira* is a wonder to behold. As a group of spectators and other *capoeira* practitioners form a circle
Line and begin to sing, clap, and play musical instruments,
(5) two ritual combatants enter the circle. They perform a fluid, acrobatic dance involving attacks, feints, and dodges. As one fighter attacks in a graceful motion (usually with a kick, leg sweep, or head butt), the other makes a countering motion to avoid the attack. All of this
(10) is improvised along with the music, making for a hypnotic, unpredictable, and utterly joyous event.

Capoeira has its roots in the dances performed by African slaves on Brazilian plantations in the 19ᵗʰ century. Because of its combat elements, the plantation
(15) owners feared that the slaves would use *capoeira* as part of a violent uprising, and the art form was banned. It was not until 1930 that Brazil legalized *capoeira*. From there, it quickly spread, becoming a popular art not just in Brazil, but also around the world.

17. In context, "fluid" (line 6) most nearly means

    (A) in a liquid state.
    (B) unstable.
    (C) stiff.
    (D) shapeless.
    (E) flowing smoothly.

18. The primary purpose of the passage is to

    (A) advocate for the legalization of *capoeira*.
    (B) contrast the relative effectiveness of several martial arts techniques.
    (C) describe a unique art form.
    (D) highlight the dangers of a violent uprising in Brazil.
    (E) provide an overview of African dance.

Homework Passage 4 (Long)

This passage provides an overview of the functions and responsibilities of the United States' Central Intelligence Agency (CIA).

The CIA's primary mission is to collect, analyze, evaluate, and disseminate foreign intelligence to assist the President and senior US Government policymakers in
Line making decisions relating to national security. This is a
(5) very complex process and involves a variety of steps.

First, we have to identify a problem or an issue of national security concern to the US Government. In some cases, the CIA is directed to study an intelligence issue— such as what activities terrorist organizations are
(10) planning, or how countries that have biological or chemical weapons plan to use these weapons—then we look for a way to collect information about the problem.

There are several ways to collect information. Translating foreign newspaper and magazine articles and
(15) radio and television broadcasts provides open-source intelligence. Imagery satellites take pictures from space, and imagery analysts write reports about what they see— for example, how many airplanes are at a foreign military base. Signals analysts work to decrypt coded messages
(20) sent by other countries. Operations officers recruit foreigners to give information about their countries.

After the information is collected, intelligence analysts pull together the relevant information from all available sources and assess what is happening, why it is
(25) happening, what might occur next, and what it means for US interests. The result of this analytic effort is timely and objective assessments, free of any political bias, provided to senior US policymakers in the form of finished intelligence products that include written reports
(30) and oral briefings.

One of these reports is the President's Daily Brief (PDB), an Intelligence Community product, which the US President and other senior officials receive each day. It is important to know that CIA analysts only report the
(35) information and do not make policy recommendations— making policy is left to agencies such as the State Department and Department of Defense. These policymakers use the information that the CIA provides to help them formulate US policy toward other countries.
(40) It is also important to know that the CIA is not a law enforcement organization. That is the job of the FBI; however, the CIA and the FBI cooperate on a number of issues, such as counterintelligence and counterterrorism. Additionally, the CIA may also engage in covert action at
(45) the President's direction and in accordance with applicable law.

The US Congress has had oversight responsibility of the CIA since the Agency was established in 1947. However, prior to the mid-1970's, oversight was less
(50) formal. The 1980 Intelligence Oversight Act charged the Senate Select Committee on Intelligence (SSCI) and the House Permanent Select Committee on Intelligence (HPSCI) with authorizing the programs of the intelligence agencies and overseeing their activities.

19. According to the passage, what is the first step in the "very complex process" (line 5)?

    (A) recruiting foreigners to give information about their countries
    (B) assessing how intelligence affects U.S. interests
    (C) providing written reports to policymakers
    (D) determining an issue to gather information about
    (E) engaging in covert actions as directed by the President

20. As it is used in the passage, the phrase "open-source" (line 15) most nearly means

    (A) easily translated.
    (B) acquired through spying.
    (C) friendly
    (D) freely available to the public.
    (E) honest

21. The third paragraph (lines 13-21) is largely concerned with

    (A) listing the most common ways in which the CIA gathers intelligence.
    (B) defining the mission of the CIA.
    (C) describing how CIA analysts formulate reports for government officials.
    (D) explaining the relationship between the CIA and Congress.
    (E) correcting misconceptions about the CIA's powers.

22. Which of the following is an example of a "finished intelligence product" (line 29)?

    (A) satellite imagery
    (B) the President's Daily Brief
    (C) translated articles from a foreign newspaper
    (D) the Intelligence Oversight Act of 1980
    (E) counterintelligence operations

23. According to the passage, what is the key difference between the CIA and the FBI?

    (A) The FBI has many more agents than the CIA.
    (B) The FBI briefs the President on key information, and the CIA argues for changes in policy.
    (C) The CIA is politically biased, while the FBI is neutral.
    (D) The CIA gathers intelligence, while the FBI enforces laws.
    (E) Only the CIA is allowed to participate in counter-terrorism operations.

24. As it is used in the passage, the word "charged" (line 50) most nearly means

    (A) formally instructed
    (B) accused
    (C) required a payment
    (D) restored electrical power
    (E) rushed forward in attack

25. The primary purpose of the passage is to

    (A) offer an overview of different ways of gathering intelligence.
    (B) advocate for a larger budget for the CIA.
    (C) contrast the functions of the CIA and the FBI.
    (D) encourage the President to take on a certain policy stance.
    (E) describe the day-to-day functions of the CIA.

Unauthorized copying or reuse of any part of this page is illegal.

SC Topic: Two-Blank Strategies (Lesson Y13a)	RC Topic: Word-in-Context Questions (Lesson Y12b)

Homework Set 1

1. When the voters realized that nearly all of the politician's answers had been -----, they became ------ and demanded that he provide more honest responses.

   (A) deceitful . . incensed
   (B) evocative . . content
   (C) precise . . enraged
   (D) elusive . . placid
   (E) bogus . . elated

2. When a flower is ------ water, its leaves will turn yellow, then turn brown, and finally shrivel up as the plant dies.

   (A) furnished with
   (B) aggregated with
   (C) conducive to
   (D) deprived of
   (E) administered

3. Allison tried to ------ her company's regulations, but they were so ------ and incomprehensible that she had difficulty following them all.

   (A) comply with . . intricate
   (B) attain . . straightforward
   (C) concede to . . apparent
   (D) evade . . perplexing
   (E) revert to . . analytical

4. When faced with ------ phenomenon, it is natural to feel somewhat ------; it is difficult to believe in what one cannot explain.

   (A) an incomprehensible . . effusive
   (B) a habitual . . skeptical
   (C) an inexplicable . . incredulous
   (D) a peculiar . . gullible
   (E) a customary . . dubious

5. The full ------ of the bank's failure was not felt immediately; many of its most damaging effects were slow to develop.

   (A) absurdity
   (B) proficiency
   (C) magnitude
   (D) reconciliation
   (E) triviality

6. The farmer's ------ attitude toward technology prevented him from using ------ new devices such as smart phones, no matter how useful they would have been to him.

   (A) provincial . . innovative
   (B) diligent . . contemporary
   (C) cognizant . . dysfunctional
   (D) primitive . . futile
   (E) vulgar . . incompetent

Unauthorized copying or reuse of any part of this page is illegal.

Version 1.3

Homework Set 2

7. The governor was truly surprised by the volume of ------ that his proposal had ------ from the citizens of his state; he had expected the plan to be quite popular.

  (A) discord . . repressed
  (B) dissent . . elicited
  (C) indifference . . generated
  (D) commendation . . provoked
  (E) amiability . . withheld

8. The eccentric inventor ------ the ------ engineering methods that he learned in school in favor of his own more unusual methods.

  (A) revoked . . bizarre
  (B) repudiated . . conventional
  (C) venerated . . predominant
  (D) circumvented . . erratic
  (E) acclaimed . . exotic

9. As part of his quest to become more ------, Didier forced himself to state his opinion clearly and confidently in at least one conversation per day.

  (A) pliable
  (B) assertive
  (C) dejected
  (D) reluctant
  (E) obedient

10. The best teachers are able to ------ important concepts both clearly and ------, since using just a few words can help facilitate the student's understanding of the concepts.

  (A) convey . . succinctly
  (B) retract . . superfluously
  (C) impart . . verbosely
  (D) relate . . expansively
  (E) inhibit . . concisely

11. The lawyer found that ------ negotiations were best handled with a ------ attitude, so as to make everyone involved more comfortable and less hostile.

  (A) combative . . malicious
  (B) soothing . . sympathetic
  (C) repulsive . . desolate
  (D) cordial . . voracious
  (E) contentious . . congenial

12. Among Mary's many ------ qualities are her intelligence, her modesty, and her unique sense of style.

  (A) transitory
  (B) adverse
  (C) awkward
  (D) laudable
  (E) virulent

Unauthorized copying or reuse of any part of this page is illegal.

Homework Passage 1 (Short)

Though the history of inter-religion relations is largely one of war and strife, there have been isolated instances of religious harmony. One of the most *Line* noteworthy of these was the kingdom of the renowned
(5) Mughal emperor, Akbar the Great, who ruled much of what is now India and Pakistan from 1556 to 1605 A.D. Though Akbar himself was born a Sunni Muslim, by the last 25 years of his reign, he was working toward bridging the gap between Sunnis and other Islamic sects.
(10) He declared that his empire would be neutral on all internal Islamic disputes, a departure from past emperors.

In addition, he worked extensively with other faiths. Many of his wives (he had nearly 40) were Hindus, as were some of his most trusted advisors. He also
(15) sponsored debates with members of many religions, including Jews, Roman Catholics, Jains, and even atheists. Akbar was so convinced by some of the Jain arguments for vegetarianism that he ceased eating meat. Toward the end of his life, he founded a new religious
(20) sect that incorporated elements of all of these religions into its belief system.

13. In the context of line 11, "departure" most nearly means

(A) project.
(B) exit.
(C) journey.
(D) differing approach.
(E) removal.

14. According to the passage, Akbar was different from most other emperors in that he

(A) was tolerant of other beliefs.
(B) feuded with rival Islamic sects.
(C) was a Muslim.
(D) started numerous wars.
(E) had many wives.

Homework Passage 2 (Short)

More than 85 percent of people with Type 2 diabetes are overweight. It is not known exactly why people who are obese are more likely to develop this disease. It may *Line* be that being overweight causes cells to change, making
(5) them resistant to the hormone insulin. Insulin carries sugar from blood to the cells, where it is used for energy. When a person is insulin-resistant, sugar cannot be transferred from blood to the cells, resulting in high blood sugar and insufficient energy to power the cells.
(10) Regions of the body with lower blood flow are particularly at risk, which is why many patients with severe diabetes must have their feet amputated.

In addition, the cells that produce insulin must work especially hard to try to keep blood sugar normal. This may cause these cells to gradually fail.

15. As it is used in line 3, "develop" most nearly means

(A) become more successful.
(B) mature.
(C) add details to.
(D) come down with.
(E) plan.

16. Which of the following statements best summarizes the main idea of the passage?

(A) Diabetes patients can take synthetic insulin to control their blood sugar levels.
(B) Overweight people are less healthy than those with average weights.
(C) Diet and exercise are the two most important factors in maintaining a healthy weight.
(D) The feet receive very little blood compared to other parts of the body.
(E) Type 2 diabetes is caused by insulin resistance, which in turn may be related to obesity.

Homework Passage 3 (Short)

The phenomenon of sound produced by rubbing a finger along the rim of a wine glass has been known since the Renaissance; Galileo even wrote about it.
Line However, it was not until the 18th century that this sound
(5) was utilized in a musical instrument. At first, the instrument was called a glass harmonica, and it consisted of a series of wine glasses filled to various levels with water. The player would rub his or her fingers on the glasses, producing an eerie yet delicate sound.

(10) Benjamin Franklin revolutionized this instrument by replacing the individual glasses with a series of glass "bowls" that were all mounted on a metal rod. As the rod spun, the player simply needed to touch the bowls to produce music. The player could thus combine sounds
(15) much more easily than before. Franklin's invention, termed the "armonica," briefly became quite popular (Mozart even composed a piece for it), but it faded from use by mid-19th century. Recently, modern and abstract musicians, who prize its distinctive, understated sound,
(20) have revived the glass harmonica.

17. In the context of the passage, "delicate" (line 9) most nearly means

   (A) awkward.
   (B) fragile.
   (C) easily offended.
   (D) subtle.
   (E) polite.

18. The main advantage of "Franklin's invention" (line 15) over earlier versions of the glass harmonica was that it

   (A) produced a strange sound.
   (B) was powered by electricity.
   (C) was much more straightforward to use.
   (D) did not rely on the friction between fingers and glass.
   (E) was stationary.

Homework Passage 4 (Long)

This passage, adapted from P.G. Wodehouse's novel My Man Jeeves, *describes the relationship between a man and his wise servant (or "man"), Jeeves.*

Jeeves—my man, you know—is really a most extraordinary chap. So capable. Honestly, I shouldn't know what to do without him. On broader lines he's like
Line those fellows who sit peering sadly at the marble walls at
(5) the Pennsylvania Station in the place marked "Inquiries." You know the fellows I mean. You go up to them and say: "When's the next train for Melonsquashville, Tennessee?" and they reply, without stopping to think, "Two-forty-three, track ten, change at San Francisco."
(10) And they're right every time. Well, Jeeves gives you just the same impression of having all the answers.

As an instance of what I mean, I remember meeting Monty Byng in Bond Street one morning, looking quite stylish in a grey check suit, and I felt I should never be
(15) happy till I had one like it. I dug the address of the tailors out of him and had them working on it inside an hour.

"Jeeves," I said that evening. "I'm getting a check suit like that one of Mr. Byng's."

"Injudicious, sir," he said firmly. "It will not become
(20) you."

"What absolute rot! It's the soundest thing I've struck for years."

"Unsuitable for you, sir."

Well, the long and the short of it was that the
(25) confounded thing came home, and I put it on, and when I caught sight of myself in the mirror I nearly fainted. Jeeves was perfectly right. I looked a cross between a music-hall comedian and a cheap bookie. Yet Monty had looked fine in absolutely the same stuff. These things are
(30) just Life's mysteries, and that's all there is to it.

But it isn't only that Jeeves's judgment about clothes is infallible, though, of course, that's really the main thing. The man knows everything. There was also that tip on the "Lincolnshire" horse race. I forget now how I got
(35) it, but it seemed to be a real, red-hot Tabasco tip.

"Jeeves," I said, for I'm fond of the man, and like to do him a good turn when I can, "if you want to make a bit of money put a bet down on the horse called Wonderchild for the 'Lincolnshire.'"

(40) He shook his head. "I'd rather not, sir."

"But it's the straight goods. I'm going to put my shirt on him."

"I do not recommend it, sir. The animal is not intended to win. Second place is what the stable is after."

(45) Perfect piffle, I thought, of course. How the deuce could Jeeves know anything about it? Still, you know what happened. Wonderchild led till almost the end, and then Banana Fritter came along and nosed him out. I went straight home and rang for Jeeves.

(50) "After this," I said, "not another step for me without your advice. From now on consider yourself the brains of the establishment."

"Very good, sir. I shall endeavor to give satisfaction."

19. Which of the following would make the best title for the passage?

(A) The Dangers of Gambling on Horse Races
(B) A Story of Two Friends
(C) Taking the Train to Melonsquashville
(D) Why I Should Listen to the Wisdom of Jeeves
(E) Wonderchild and Banana Fritter

20. Jeeves proves his good judgment on issues of fashion by

(A) declaring that the narrator should bet his shirt on a horse race.
(B) telling the narrator to dress more like a music-hall comedian.
(C) giving the narrator the address of a good tailor's shop.
(D) revealing the time of the next train to Tennessee.
(E) advising the narrator not to wear a grey check suit.

21. As it is used in the passage, the word "become" (line 20) most nearly means

(A) turn into.
(B) be socially acceptable for.
(C) grow up to be.
(D) happen to.
(E) look stylish on.

22. What is an example of one of "Life's mysteries," according to the narrator?

(A) how a horse named "Wonderchild" could lose a race
(B) how a servant could know which train to take
(C) how one man can look good in a suit while another man looks awful in the same suit
(D) how people can lose money gambling on horse races
(E) how Jeeves could be so ungrateful as to not take his advice

23. In line 38, the phrase "a good turn" most nearly means

(A) a beneficial change in direction
(B) a helpful act
(C) a wonderful transformation
(D) a brilliant plot twist
(E) a pleasant rotation

24. What does the narrator mean when he says "I'm going to put my shirt on him" (lines 42-43)?

(A) He is going to bet as much as he can on the horse called Wonderchild.
(B) He is very angry at the man who gave him the poor tip for the horse race.
(C) He is going to have Jeeves try on a new shirt.
(D) He is giving his old clothes to Monty Byng.
(E) He is going to help design the horse's outfit.

25. What was the outcome of the Lincolnshire horse race?

(A) Wonderchild finished dead last.
(B) Banana Fritter won, barely beating Wonderchild.
(C) Banana Fritter finished first, and the narrator won his bet.
(D) Wonderchild finished first, and the narrator won his bet.
(E) Wonderchild won, but the narrator did not bet on the race.

Unauthorized copying or reuse of any part of this page is illegal.

Version 1.3

Y14HW: Homework and Extra Practice

SC Topic: Two-Blank Strategies (Lesson Y13a)	**RC Topic**: Main Idea Questions (Lesson Y14b)

Homework Set 1

1. The mayor did his best to ------ the angry citizens, but in the end his assurances could not quiet their vocal ------.

   (A) incense . . timidity
   (B) placate . . dissent
   (C) infuriate . . incredulity
   (D) circumvent . . compassion
   (E) appease . . tranquility

2. Numerous environmental groups have ------ the proposed plan to build a new air- and water-polluting coal plant.

   (A) condemned
   (B) acclaimed
   (C) augmented
   (D) venerated
   (E) conceded

3. The letter of apology was ------ sign in the relationship between the feuding neighbors, who now could begin to hope for a ------.

   (A) a conducive . . dejection
   (B) a perplexing . . pliability
   (C) an auspicious . . reconciliation
   (D) a reclusive . . aggregation
   (E) a cordial . . denunciation

4. In order to ------ his reputation, the disgraced actor spent a large amount of time volunteering for women's shelters and other ------ causes.

   (A) salvage . . desolate
   (B) attain . . repulsive
   (C) redeem . . benevolent
   (D) detract from . . humanitarian
   (E) indict . . wicked

5. Though trained chimpanzees seem ------ on television, they can never be fully tamed.

   (A) docile
   (B) ruthless
   (C) feral
   (D) juvenile
   (E) voracious

6. I chose Ms. Gutierrez as my lawyer because she is ------ at constructing persuasive arguments but also because she is skilled at ------ the claims of opposing lawyers.

   (A) incompetent . . rebutting
   (B) capable . . complying with
   (C) discordant . . asserting
   (D) proficient . . refuting
   (E) elusive . . mandating

Unauthorized copying or reuse of any part of this page is illegal.

C2 education
be smarter.

Homework Set 2

7. The speaker tried to ------ the crowd to oppose the government, saying that most politicians were ------ people who were actively trying to harm ordinary citizens.

   (A) spur . . negligible
   (B) alleviate . . spiteful
   (C) rouse . . amiable
   (D) soothe . . benign
   (E) incite . . malicious

8. Rather than continue to complain about his punishment, the teenager chose to ------ his parents' decision.

   (A) repudiate
   (B) abide by
   (C) overlook
   (D) revoke
   (E) disregard

9. With a ------ tone in his voice, the former thief promised his family that he would never steal again and that he would not ------ his old, criminal habits.

   (A) resolute . . revert to
   (B) feeble . . relapse to
   (C) resilient . . shun
   (D) vulnerable . . proceed from
   (E) cowardly . . evade

10. Rather than create newer, even more ------ technologies, the company became ------ with its success, stopped making progress, and began losing business.

   (A) contentious . . transitory
   (B) inventive . . sorrowful
   (C) outdated . . laudable
   (D) innovative . . complacent
   (E) conventional . . content

11. The skyscraper was built to ------ even the most severe tremors, so the minor earthquake did not harm it at all.

   (A) withstand
   (B) evoke
   (C) retract
   (D) exaggerate
   (E) dissect

12. The professor's lecture was both ------ and ------, as it shifted topics often and went on well past its scheduled ending time.

   (A) rambling . . protracted
   (B) relevant . . genuine
   (C) sprawling . . succinct
   (D) verbose . . concise
   (E) fleeting . . prolonged

Unauthorized copying or reuse of any part of this page is illegal.

Version 1.3

Homework Passage 1 (Short)

Today, the terms "Internet" and "World Wide Web" are often used interchangeably. They are quite different concepts, however. The Internet was created in 1969 by
Line the Advanced Research Projects Agency (ARPA, now
(5) DARPA), a part of the United States Department of Defense. It was designed to allow communication between universities and government offices so that a single system failure or attack could not disrupt the free flow of information. It was used for electronic mail and
(10) file transfer. For twenty years, the Internet grew, but it remained little known and was rarely used by the public.

That all changed with the advent of the World Wide Web. The Web was first conceptualized by the British computer scientist Tim Berners-Lee in 1989, and first
(15) implemented in 1991. Its main innovation was the creation of a series of "hypertext" documents that could link to each other and be read by anyone with a computer and a web browser. The Web quickly grew in terms of both number of users and amount of information
(20) contained, to the point that the Web and the Internet now threaten to replace or marginalize nearly all forms of traditional media.

13. According to the passage, the original function of the Internet was to

(A) develop a more efficient and robust form of communication for universities and the government.
(B) replace traditional forms of media such as the newspaper and the record album.
(C) provide a new source of entertainment.
(D) create a vast resource of information for the general public.
(E) allow people from different locations to interact in unusual ways.

14. Which of the following most clearly states the main idea of the passage?

(A) The Internet and the World Wide Web are exactly the same.
(B) The World Wide Web helped the Internet become more popular and widespread.
(C) The United States government played a key role in the development of the Internet.
(D) The Internet was created as a series of "hypertext" documents.
(E) Soon after its creation, the Internet revolutionized the lives of average people around the world

     Unauthorized copying or reuse of any part of this page is illegal.

Homework Passage 2 (Short)

Science can be dangerous work. One of the most famous examples is the life of Marie Skłodowska-Curie, the pioneering scientist who helped discover the elements
Line radium and polonium. Both elements are noteworthy for
(5) their radioactivity (a term that Skłodowska-Curie herself coined), but at the time of her studies, Skłodowska-Curie knew nothing of the deleterious health effects that can result from exposure to radioactive elements. A prolonged (and casual—she often walked around with
(10) radium samples in her coat pocket) exposure to radioactive substances eventually led to her death from cancer in 1934. Today, Skłodowska-Curie's original papers are so radioactive that those who wish to read them must put on protective suits. Even her cookbooks
(15) are considered too dangerous to handle!

15. One can conclude from the passage that the effects of radioactivity on the human body are

   (A) damaging but brief.
   (B) entirely benign.
   (C) occasionally therapeutic.
   (D) both helpful and harmful.
   (E) destructive and enduring.

16. Which of the following would make the best title for the passage?

   (A) The Discovery of Polonium
   (B) Famous Women in Science
   (C) A Foolish Scientist
   (D) Cooking with Marie Curie
   (E) A Radioactive Life (and Death)

Homework Passage 3 (Short)

This passage is from The Life and Times of Frederick Douglass, *the autobiography of the educator and activist, who began life as a slave.*

I have often been asked, how I felt when first I found myself on free soil. And my readers may share the same curiosity. There is scarcely anything in my experience
Line about which I could not give a more satisfactory answer.
(5) A new world had opened upon me. If life is more than breath, and the 'quick round of blood,' I lived more in one day than in a year of my slave life. It was a time of joyous excitement that words can but tamely describe. In a letter written to a friend soon after reaching New York,
(10) I said: 'I felt as one might feel upon escape from a den of hungry lions.' Anguish and grief, like darkness and rain, may be depicted; but gladness and joy, like the rainbow, defy the skill of pen or pencil.

17. The primary purpose of the passage is to

   (A) attempt to describe the overwhelming emotions of a life-changing moment.
   (B) urge others to stop asking him about a traumatic event.
   (C) tell about a journey to an unfamiliar place.
   (D) denounce the evils of slavery.
   (E) praise the bravery of escaped slaves.

18. According to the author of the passage, positive emotions are "like the rainbow" (line 12) in that

   (A) they always occur after a period of darkness.
   (B) they disappear shortly after they are first created.
   (C) one cannot anticipate when they will end.
   (D) they can be difficult to adequately express in words.
   (E) they seem to have many different parts.

Unauthorized copying or reuse of any part of this page is illegal.   Version 1.3

Homework Passage 4 (Long)

This passage describes how officials use computers to fight widespread disease outbreaks, or "pandemics," such as the 2009 H1N1 (swine flu) outbreak.

Just months after the first cases of swine flu appeared in April 2009, millions of Americans had gotten sick and some had even died. By the end of the
Line year, the virus had spread worldwide, creating the first
(5) influenza pandemic since 1968.

As drug companies produced a vaccine that prevented millions more from catching this flu, researchers participating in an international project called MIDAS were simulating disease spread. The simulations
(10) let them explore how the pandemic might unfold, who was more likely to get sick and which interventions might protect the most people. The results helped inform public policy decisions.

To create the pandemic flu simulations, the MIDAS
(15) researchers use computer models to build virtual cities, countries and even continents. Here, thousands of pretend people go to school, work, stores and other places. The researchers base the residents' activities on information about actual people like you.
(20) Stephen Eubank, a physicist at Virginia Tech University in Blacksburg and part of the MIDAS team, has modeled virtual versions of major U.S. metropolitan areas using local transportation and census data. In Eubank's cities, there really are six (or fewer) degrees of
(25) separation between any two people—making it easy for germs to spread.

"Viruses don't care much about geography," says Eubank. "They care about social networks and how people come into contact with each other."
(30) Another key part of studying the spread of infection with computers involves developing a virtual version of the germ. To model its spread as realistically as possible, the researchers track down everything known about the infectious agent. Eubank, who has studied plague,
(35) smallpox and anthrax, has gathered information on how each agent spreads between people, how contagious it is and how long it takes for an infected person to show symptoms.

With all the modeling pieces in place, the MIDAS
(40) researchers invite policymakers to ask questions that can be answered using the models. Questions range from *What happens if we don't do anything?* to *How many people could be protected if we intervene?*

The researchers create different simulations that
(45) change the variables, like the contagiousness of the virus or the number of people taking "snow days"—Eubank's term for people who voluntarily hang out at home to avoid infection.

"What's so great about the computer simulations is
(50) that you can try out different situations that you can't create in real societies," says Eubank.

With more than 250 possible combinations to simulate, Eubank says he relies on statisticians to help him determine which arrangements will produce the most
(55) informative results.

"It's easy to come up with questions," says Mills. "The hard part is figuring out which ones we should—and could—answer."

Because of the amount of data and calculations
(60) involved, the simulations run on high-performance computers that can simulate a 180-day outbreak in a matter of hours. Eubank uses software programs to take snapshots of the pretend pandemic as it occurs.

"I know exactly when a virtual person gets infected,
(65) shows symptoms and recovers," says Eubank, explaining that the computer records every change in disease state.

Eubank and other researchers modeling 2009 H1N1 pandemic flu have simulated outbreak scenarios in communities across the United States. The results
(70) suggested that early vaccination of school kids best reduced disease spread, while vaccinating elders became more important later on. The simulations also indicated that people at risk for serious complications—like pregnant women or individuals with pre-existing health
(75) problems—should be given antiviral medicines to take at the first signs of illness.

While the results generated by the simulations are useful, Eubank stresses that they're not a guarantee of what actually will happen. He and others often will ask
(80) different models the same questions and, when the models agree, they'll have more confidence in the predictions.

19. Which of the following would make the best title for the passage?

(A) The History of Swine Flu
(B) Six Degrees of Separation
(C) Exploring Virtual Cities
(D) How Disease Influences Public Policy
(E) Simulating a Pandemic

20. According to the passage, the MIDAS computer simulations did all of the following EXCEPT

(A) determine which actions could best prevent the disease's spread.
(B) help governmental leaders decide how to fight the disease.
(C) help create a vaccine to prevent people from catching the disease.
(D) describe how the disease would probably spread.
(E) identify the people who were most at risk from the disease.

Unauthorized copying or reuse of any part of this page is illegal.

21. Throughout the passage, the word "models" is used to mean

(A) people who pose for painters, sculptors, and other artists
(B) particular versions of a product, used to demonstrate the product's features
(C) excellent examples of an ideal quality
(D) people who are paid to wear clothes in fashion shows and magazines
(E) simplified versions of something used to analyze and solve problems

22. The sixth paragraph (lines 30-38) is primarily concerned with describing

(A) the professional qualifications of Stephen Eubank.
(B) the computer hardware and software used to perform the simulations.
(C) the various characteristics of a disease that can affect how it spreads.
(D) the results of the MIDAS study.
(E) the differences between plague, smallpox, and anthrax.

23. What is the meaning of the phrase "snow days" (line 46) as it is used in the passage?

(A) days when there is a particularly heavy snowfall
(B) days when people spend more time outside because the television reception is poor
(C) days when people avoid going out so as to not contract a disease
(D) days when the sky is filled with fluffy white clouds
(E) days when children get to stay home from school because of inclement weather

24. According to Eubank, what is one of the foremost advantages of a computer simulation?

(A) results that are guaranteed to be accurate
(B) the ease with which researchers can determine which questions can and should be answered
(C) inexpensive equipment
(D) the ability to test many different scenarios, not just the ones that have occurred in real life
(E) eliminating the need for vaccinations

25. One can infer from the MIDAS group's results (lines 69-76) that which of the following groups is at the least risk of infection from the H1N1 flu?

(A) school-age children
(B) healthy, middle-aged adults
(C) people who already have health problems
(D) the elderly
(E) pregnant women

26. Which of the following questions could the MIDAS simulation best answer?

(A) Which age group should receive the first round of vaccinations?
(B) How do computer models work?
(C) How can scientists find a cure for smallpox?
(D) When will the next pandemic occur?
(E) What are the side effects of a swine flu vaccination?

27. The primary purpose of the passage is to

(A) list the symptoms and causes of the H1N1 flu.
(B) criticize cities for inadequately funding programs that fight pandemics.
(C) illustrate the day-to-day activities of a public health researcher.
(D) tell about several potential uses for computer technology in the future.
(E) describe an innovative new technique for combating a public health problem.

Unauthorized copying or reuse of any part of this page is illegal.   Version 1.3

Y15HW: Homework and Extra Practice

SC Topic: Tone Strategies (Lesson Y15a)	**RC Topic**: Main Idea Questions (Lesson Y14b)

Homework Set 1

1. When she first moved into the city, Harriet lived in an apartment that was so ------ that she could walk its entire length in three steps.

   (A) expansive
   (B) luxurious
   (C) superfluous
   (D) minuscule
   (E) magnificent

2. Rather than continue the policies started under his ------, the new manager ------ the company's original guidelines.

   (A) antecedent . . lapsed to
   (B) descendant . . prolonged
   (C) benefactor . . altered
   (D) predecessor . . reverted to
   (E) villain . . maintained

3. Marcus' ------ about his upcoming speech was so strong that he began to sweat and stutter.

   (A) apprehension
   (B) malice
   (C) persistence
   (D) poise
   (E) cordiality

4. In order to preserve the surprise, Arushi planned the party ------, even using a disguise so that she would not be recognized.

   (A) transparently
   (B) auspiciously
   (C) obliviously
   (D) covertly
   (E) sincerely

5. The soft drink company made all of its employees agree not to ------ the secret recipes of its products.

   (A) salvage
   (B) disclose
   (C) conceal
   (D) commend
   (E) abide

6. Over a billion people worldwide are forced to ------ flimsy huts in overcrowded slums because they are too ------ to afford better housing.

   (A) reside in . . prosperous
   (B) shun . . depleted
   (C) circumvent . . complacent
   (D) inhabit . . destitute
   (E) revoke . . wealthy

Unauthorized copying or reuse of any part of this page is illegal.

Homework Set 2

7. Although when he was younger, he was ------ toward those less educated that himself, today Yao is much more respectful of their abilities.

   (A) congenial
   (B) contemptuous
   (C) assertive
   (D) flattering
   (E) sympathetic

8. In ------ attempt to ------ the damage caused by the fire, neighbors tried to douse the flames with garden hoses; the fire continued to spread, however.

   (A) an adequate . . alleviate
   (B) an ambivalent . . retract
   (C) a futile . . mitigate
   (D) a fruitless . . incite
   (E) a competent . . impair

9. After finishing the ------, 20-mile hike, Fiorello was so ------ that he collapsed into bed and did not move until morning.

   (A) taxing . . vigorous
   (B) elementary . . fatigued
   (C) laborious . . lively
   (D) leisurely . . assertive
   (E) grueling . . weary

10. Keiko could understand why people believed in aliens, but she considered tales of alien abductions to be ------.

   (A) sensible
   (B) commonplace
   (C) inexplicable
   (D) incessant
   (E) rational

11. Laura does not enjoy paying taxes, but she ------ those who avoid doing so, for she considers it a duty that should not be evaded.

   (A) acclaims
   (B) elicits
   (C) deplores
   (D) persuades
   (E) placates

12. Elbert will never forget the events of that day; they are firmly ------ his memory.

   (A) expelled from
   (B) reclusive from
   (C) dubious in
   (D) transitory in
   (E) embedded in

Unauthorized copying or reuse of any part of this page is illegal.   Version 1.3

Homework Passage 1 (Short Paired)

Passage 1:

Today, writers in most countries take for granted the freedom to write whatever they like without fear of political reprisals from their governments. However, this
Line freedom does not as yet extend to all nations. Most
(5) prominently, China places severe restrictions on its authors and journalists, even going so far as to repeatedly imprison some of those who advocate against government policies.

One of the most prominent opponents of these
(10) repressive policies in Communist China is Liu Xiaobo, a renowned intellectual, author, and civil rights activist. For decades, Liu has spoken out in favor of a freer China in his writings; he also participated in the writing of the "Charter 08," a document that calls for a remaking of the
(15) Chinese government to allow free speech, association, and religion, as well as many other reforms. As a result of this, Liu was imprisoned for the fourth time. In 2010, while still incarcerated, he was awarded the Nobel Peace Prize for his efforts.

Passage 2:

(20) Throughout history, writers who have openly criticized their governments have often been punished, particularly by authoritarian regimes. In Communist-era Russia, thousands of writers were exiled, imprisoned in *gulags* (labor camps notorious for their poor conditions),
(25) or killed. The famous novelist Aleksandr Solzhenitsyn, after serving an eight-year sentence in these *gulags*, brought their inhumane conditions to the attention of the outside world with his novel *One Day in the Life of Ivan Denisovich* and his non-fiction treatise *Gulag*
(30) *Archipelago*. For writing these works, he was forced into exile in 1974, only returning to his native land 20 years later, after the fall of the Communist regime.

Other writers have paid an even greater price for expressing their discontent. During the French
(35) Revolution, the noted feminist and playwright Olympe de Gouges was executed for attacking the revolutionary government's poor treatment of women and continued use of slave labor. Though women would not gain equal rights in France until the 20th century, she is remembered
(40) fondly today for her enlightened attitudes and her iron will.

13. The primary purpose of Passage 1 is to describe

  (A) one man's fight against his country's repressive policies.
  (B) a few ways in which China has changed in the past few decades.
  (C) the gains attained by civil rights activists around the world.
  (D) the fundamental rights guaranteed by most nations.
  (E) the criteria for awarding the Nobel Peace Prize.

14. The author of Passage 2 describes "Olympe de Gouges" (line 35) with a tone of

  (A) contempt.
  (B) anxiety.
  (C) esteem.
  (D) satire.
  (E) disinterest.

15. According to information in the passages, what does "Liu Xiaobo" (line 10, Passage 1) have in common with "Alexandr Solzhenitsyn" (line 25, Passage 2)?

  (A) Both are famous novelists.
  (B) Both fought primarily for an end to slave labor.
  (C) Both were imprisoned by Communist governments.
  (D) Both won a Nobel Peace Prize.
  (E) Both were forced into exile for a long period of time.

16. The two passages differ in that Passage 1 focuses more on

  (A) gender and racial equality.
  (B) writers who have been executed by their governments.
  (C) Soviet-era Russia.
  (D) criticism of repressive governments.
  (E) recent events.

Unauthorized copying or reuse of any part of this page is illegal.

Homework Passage 2 (Short)

Over 2,000 years ago, the ancient Greeks built computers. Not computers as we think of them today (in other words, not *digital* computers), but amazingly
Line complex devices nonetheless. One such device, known as
(5) the Antikythera mechanism, contained around 37 gears and could be used to make complicated astronomical calculations, including the positions of the sun and moon, times of eclipses, phases of the moon, and much more. It could also account for leap years, even though it was
(10) created before the first calendar that incorporated this concept. All the gears and dials were combined in a compact package that was designed to be transported easily from place to place.

The Antikythera mechanism was discovered as part
(15) of an ancient shipwreck in the Mediterranean Sea in 1900, but archaeologists were not able to determine its function for almost 50 years. Gradually, researchers realized the device's purpose and astounding craftsmanship. Today, scientists estimate that the
(20) mechanism, which was built around 100 B.C.E., was not surpassed technologically for 1800 years.

17. The author's attitude toward the makers of the "Antikythera mechanism" (line 5) can best be described as

(A) distressed.
(B) neutral.
(C) childish.
(D) astonished.
(E) lenient.

18. The primary purpose of the passage is most likely to

(A) argue that ancient Greek technology was the most sophisticated of all time.
(B) tell how to make complicated astronomical calculations.
(C) chronicle the history of non-digital computers.
(D) list the most important historical shipwrecks.
(E) describe an innovative ancient invention.

Homework Passage 3 (Long)

The following passage, written in 2003, examines how the classes that high school students take can affect their futures.

A growing body of literature suggests that high school curriculum, especially during the senior year, is greatly lacking in academic intensity. A recent report
Line from the National Commission on the High School
(5) Senior Year indicates that students find the last year of high school to be "a waste of time" and "boring." Not only are students not being challenged during their senior year, they are also not preparing for college. The Education Trust reports that while almost three-quarters
(10) of high school graduates are entering higher education each year, only about half of these students have completed at least a mid-level college preparatory curriculum (4 years of English, and 3 years each of math, science, and social studies), and these numbers drop to
(15) about 12 percent when 2 years of foreign language and a semester of computer science are included.

Rather than using the final high school year to prepare for college, an increasing number of seniors are studying less and electing to take less demanding
(20) courses. According to a recent study, this "senior slump" is due in part to higher education institutions failing to provide sufficient incentives for seniors to complete challenging coursework. College admissions decisions do not depend on second-semester courses or grades.
(25) Additionally, community colleges often send weak signals to high school students about the preparations they need to make in order to succeed in college—only when students arrive for orientation or registration are they informed that they must pass placement exams
(30) before they are allowed to take credit courses.

A wasted senior year of high school can result in negative social and economic consequences for students during college. Research indicates that students who waste their senior year, even if they engaged in
(35) challenging courses during their preceding years of high school, are often unprepared for college-level work and are more likely to drop-out. These claims are supported by recent studies by the National Center for Education Statistics (NCES). According to one study, the strongest
(40) predictor of whether a student gains a bachelor's degree is the level of academic rigor of his or her secondary education, and another study found that three years after entering a 4-year postsecondary institution, 87 percent of those students who had completed rigorous coursework
(45) in high school had persisted and remained continuously enrolled at a 4-year college or university, whereas only 62 percent of students who had not taken rigorous secondary coursework did the same.

The consequences of "senior slump" are also
(50) reflected in the rising numbers of students who must take remedial courses. Recent figures compiled by the NCES show that nearly half of all 4-year college students are required to complete at least one remedial course, and the Bridge Project at Stanford University estimates that over
(55) half of the students entering community colleges directly

Unauthorized copying or reuse of any part of this page is illegal.   Version 1.3

from high school do not meet the placement exam standards. Among those requiring remediation are students who took rigorous courses during their early years of high school, but because they wasted their senior *(60)* year, forgot what they had previously learned. These students waste time and money by having to repeat topics they studied in high school instead of moving on to college-level work.

19. Which of the following titles best describes the passage?

   (A) How to Improve Community Colleges
   (B) The Effects of "The Senior Slump"
   (C) Are Enough Students Entering College?
   (D) Comparing the High School Curriculums of Developed Nations
   (E) Why Students Should Take More Computer Courses

20. According to the passage, why do high school students often find their senior years to be "a waste of time" (line 6)?

   (A) They would rather be taking fewer college-preparatory classes and more "fun" classes.
   (B) The coursework is neither challenging nor important.
   (C) They are planning on dropping out of college.
   (D) They believe that they are being forced to study too hard.
   (E) Most of them will not be attending college at all.

21. The first paragraph of the passage (lines 1-16) is primarily focused on

   (A) stating the basic characteristics of the "senior slump."
   (B) describing the harmful effects of failing placement exams.
   (C) comparing students who take difficult courses for all four years to those who do not.
   (D) identifying some of the causes of the "senior slump."
   (E) illustrating how a high school curriculum can affect how long a student stays in college.

22. Which of the following factors does the passage identify as one of the causes of the "senior slump"?

   (A) the laziness of most high school students
   (B) a new emphasis on earning money at after-school jobs
   (C) the poor course selection available at most high schools
   (D) the lack of weight that colleges place on the courses students take during the senior year
   (E) parents encouraging their students to take easier classes

23. What is the meaning of "orientation" (line 28) as it is used in the passage?

   (A) a person's inborn preference
   (B) the way a group of objects are arranged
   (C) the main focus of an essay or article
   (D) a formal introduction to a new environment
   (E) the direction in which a person is facing

24. According to the passage, what is the most important factor in determining students' success in college?

   (A) their grades during the senior year
   (B) their extracurricular activities
   (C) their standardized test scores
   (D) the difficulty of their high school coursework
   (E) the number of math courses they take during their first three years of high school

25. Which of the following is NOT a common consequence of the "senior slump"?

   (A) failing placement exams at a higher rate
   (B) wasting money and time on remedial courses
   (C) being unprepared for college-level courses
   (D) dropping out of college at a higher rate
   (E) taking more foreign-language courses

26. The primary purpose of the passage is to

   (A) praise students for taking easier courses in their senior year of high school.
   (B) show the importance of taking foreign-language courses.
   (C) argue that fewer students should attend college.
   (D) analyze a problem and some of its harmful effects.
   (E) prove that test scores are a better measure of future success than the difficulty of coursework.

Unauthorized copying or reuse of any part of this page is illegal.

| **SC Topic**: Using Tone (Lesson Y15a) | **RC Topic**: Inference Questions (Lesson Y16b) |

Homework Set 1

1. In order to ------ her goal of being a professional cellist, Marta practiced over 10 hours per day.

   (A) attain
   (B) restrain
   (C) evade
   (D) deflect
   (E) revoke

4. Although he was generally ------ and quiet, Paul could become quite forceful and ------ when discussing his favorite subject, action movies.

   (A) submissive . . effusive
   (B) assertive . . incoherent
   (C) bold . . verbose
   (D) timid . . modest
   (E) docile . . methodical

2. Knowing that either a 'yes' or a 'no' answer would ------ his already angry constituents, the senator chose instead to give a more ------ answer.

   (A) incite . . equivocal
   (B) soothe . . definitive
   (C) placate . . ambivalent
   (D) incense . . malicious
   (E) laud . . discordant

5. Rather than be ------ and file a lawsuit, Gina chose to forgive her doctor for misdiagnosing her.

   (A) reconciliatory
   (B) gracious
   (C) conducive
   (D) vindictive
   (E) congenial

3. The teacher tried to ------ her students into doing a science fair project by offering them extra credit for doing one.

   (A) abide
   (B) prod
   (C) withstand
   (D) decay
   (E) circumvent

6. Though a billion dollars sounds like a lot of money, it is actually ------ amount compared to the total United States budget.

   (A) a complacent
   (B) an intricate
   (C) a monumental
   (D) a vast
   (E) a negligible

Unauthorized copying or reuse of any part of this page is illegal.

Version 1.3

Homework Set 2

7. By the time the CD was invented, the 8-track cassette was already becoming out of date; today, it is completely ------.

   (A) innovative
   (B) amiable
   (C) obsolete
   (D) contemporary
   (E) incessant

8. Before her first show at an art gallery, Juana was quite ------, but her nervousness quickly dissolved when she heard some of the ------ that her work was receiving.

   (A) apprehensive . . acclaim
   (B) decisive . . denunciation
   (C) agitation . . perplexity
   (D) upbeat . . indictment
   (E) composed . . commendation

9. The student's comment was intriguing, but the professor chose not to ------ it further because it was not ------ the subject of the day's discussion.

   (A) detract from . . relevant to
   (B) dissent from . . cognizant of
   (C) converse about . . pertinent to
   (D) elicit . . auspicious for
   (E) refute . . foreign to

10. Despite many setbacks, Abdul remained ------, and he persisted until he graduated from college.

    (A) pliable
    (B) impartial
    (C) resolute
    (D) elusive
    (E) dejected

11. Normally a free spender, Alana was forced to become more ------ when she lost her high-paying job.

    (A) ample
    (B) extravagant
    (C) cordial
    (D) frugal
    (E) superfluous

12. Though the lawyer doubted the ------ of his client's claims, he had no choice but to present them as if they were true.

    (A) resilience
    (B) incredulity
    (C) adversity
    (D) destitution
    (E) veracity

Unauthorized copying or reuse of any part of this page is illegal.

Homework Passage 1 (Short)

One of the most remarkable citizen-led movements of recent years is the Women of Liberia Mass Action for Peace movement (WLMAP). Liberia, the West African
Line nation that was colonized in the early 1800s by freed
(5) American slaves, has had a tumultuous history. Most recently, the country was wracked by uprisings and civil war for more than two decades, starting in 1980. By the early 2000s, many women in Liberia were fed up with the instability, violence, and loss of essential freedoms.
(10) Led by social worker Leymah Gbowee, groups of Christian and Muslim women united to stage non-violent protests calling for peace, fair elections, and the resignation of dictator Charles Taylor.

Eventually, the WLMAP forced Taylor to agree to
(15) peace talks in neighboring Ghana, then staged a sit-in around the talks so that none of the parties could leave until peace was achieved. As a result, Liberia's civil war ended, Taylor was forced into exile (and later brought to trial for war crimes), and an election was held. Fittingly,
(20) the winner of the election was a woman: Ellen Johnson Sirleaf, the first female head of state of an African nation.

13. The passage implies that the WLMAP called for "the resignation of dictator Charles Taylor" (lines 12-13) because

   (A) he agreed to a cease-fire at peace talks in Ghana.
   (B) he had violated the civil rights of his citizens.
   (C) they disapproved of his stances on economic issues.
   (D) he was not a Christian.
   (E) he was implicated in a bribery scandal.

14. The WLMAP's "non-violent protests" (lines 11-12) proved to be

   (A) largely counterproductive.
   (B) dangerous and unrewarding.
   (C) overwhelmingly successful.
   (D) noble but useless.
   (E) occasionally effective.

Homework Passage 2 (Short)

Not all forests are located in warm or wet environments. In fact, huge numbers of trees thrive in Canada, Alaska, Russia, and other extreme northern
Line regions. These regions, which experience little rainfall
(5) and long, frigid winters, are collectively called "taiga." More than a quarter of the world's forestland is classified as taiga, making it the world's largest land biome. Most of the plant life in the taiga consists of conifers (trees that bear cones), including spruce, fir, and pine. These trees
(10) have come up with some remarkable adaptations to their harsh environment. Their narrow shape and downward-drooping branches allow them to shed snow; they have shallow roots because of the thin soil layer; and some even harden their bark in the winter as a protective
(15) measure. Such adjustments allow these impressive trees to survive well north of the Arctic Circle, in areas where few humans dare to go.

15. In context, "bear" (line 9) most nearly means

   (A) endorse.
   (B) endure.
   (C) push down on.
   (D) produce.
   (E) communicate.

16. The passage implies that which of the following statements is true?

   (A) Over half of the world's trees are contained in the taiga.
   (B) Trees without deep root systems cannot survive in the Arctic Circle.
   (C) Most taiga is located in the southern hemisphere.
   (D) Trees with harder barks are better equipped to survive in cold weather.
   (E) The taiga is one of the three wettest biomes on Earth.

Unauthorized copying or reuse of any part of this page is illegal.

Version 1.3

Homework Passage 3 (Short)

In 1938, the United States Congress passed the Fair Labor Standards Act (FLSA). This law established a federal minimum wage for most workers, guaranteed
Line extra pay for overtime work, and outlawed dangerous
(5) child labor. The minimum wage was set at $0.25 per hour (about $3.85 in today's dollars).

Prior to the passage of the FLSA, most states did not have minimum wage laws, which forced workers to bargain with their employers in the hopes of establishing
(10) a fair wage. Since most workers of the day toiled in low-skill industries like manufacturing, they were easily replaced if their wage demands grew too high. This meant that the employers had far more leverage in wage negotiations than did the employees, even when the
(15) employees banded together in a labor union. The FLSA was one of the first laws to attempt to correct this imbalance of power and give employees a greater chance of earning a living wage.

17. One can infer from that passage that, before the FLSA was passed

(A) the minimum wage was higher than $0.25 per hour.
(B) all laborers were paid less than a living wage.
(C) labor unions were nonexistent.
(D) children worked in hazardous conditions in some areas.
(E) employers had very little leverage in wage negotiations.

18. The passage implies that workers in "industries like manufacturing" (line 11) were especially vulnerable to low wages because they

(A) were lazy and apathetic.
(B) could not form labor unions.
(C) refused to work overtime.
(D) often had not finished high school.
(E) could be easily replaced by other low-skill workers.

Homework Passage 4 (Long)

This passage describes the history, unique characteristics, and popularity of coffee.

Civilization in its onward march has produced only three important brewed beverages—tea, coffee, and hot cocoa. Though all three are popular around the world,
Line coffee has a unique place in the hearts of people
(5) everywhere.

Coffee is universal in its appeal. All nations show it respect. It has become recognized as a human necessity. It is no longer a luxury or an indulgence; it is a key component of human energy and human efficiency.
(10) People love coffee because of its two-fold effect—the pleasurable sensation and the increased efficiency it produces.

Coffee has an important place in the diet of all the civilized peoples of earth. It is a democratic beverage.
(15) Not only is it the drink of fashionable society, but it is also a favorite beverage of the men and women who do the world's work, whether they toil with brain or brawn. It has been acclaimed "the most grateful lubricant known to the human machine," and "the most delightful taste in
(20) all nature."

No "food drink" has ever encountered so much opposition as coffee. Given to the world by the church and dignified by the medical profession, nevertheless it has had to suffer from religious superstition and medical
(25) prejudice. During the thousand years of its development it has experienced fierce political opposition, stupid fiscal restrictions, unjust taxes, irksome duties; but, surviving all of these, it has triumphantly moved on to a foremost place in the catalog of popular beverages.

(30) But coffee is something more than a beverage. It is one of the world's most helpful foods. There are other foods that make us feel better, but none that excels it for taste and beneficial effects, the psychology of which is to be found in its unique flavor and aroma. Men and women
(35) drink coffee because it adds to their sense of well-being. It not only smells good and tastes good to all mankind, but all respond to its wonderful stimulating properties.

The chief factors in coffee's goodness are the caffeine content and the caffeol. Caffeine supplies the
(40) principal stimulant. It increases the capacity for muscular and mental work without harmful reaction. The caffeol supplies the flavor and the aroma—that indescribable Oriental fragrance that woos us through the nostrils, forming one of the principal elements that make up the
(45) lure of coffee. There are several other constituents, including certain innocuous so-called caffetannic acids, that, in combination with the caffeol, give the beverage its rare flavor and appeal.

Version 1.3

Unauthorized copying or reuse of any part of this page is illegal.

19. The passage implies that coffee is "a human necessity" (line 7) because it

    (A) has a long and interesting history
    (B) allows people to work for longer and with greater energy
    (C) can be served hot or over ice
    (D) was first discovered by figures in the Church
    (E) tastes very good

20. What is the "two-fold effect" (line 10) of coffee?

    (A) it pleases the senses and stimulates the mind
    (B) it causes both superstition and medical opposition
    (C) it has an Oriental fragrance and helps to build muscle
    (D) it relaxes the mind and causes sleepiness
    (E) it incurs excessive taxes and unfair restrictions

21. According to the passage, what types of people drink coffee?

    (A) only the members of high society
    (B) only people who work with their hands
    (C) all people everywhere
    (D) all people in America, but not many people elsewhere
    (E) mostly men

22. One can infer that coffee has overcome which of the following obstacles?

    (A) incomparable appeal
    (B) unpleasant smell
    (C) poor taste
    (D) restrictions imposed by governments
    (E) harmful health effects

23. According to the passage, what makes coffee "more than a beverage" (line 30)?

    (A) It is more popular than tea or hot cocoa.
    (B) It was given to the world by religious figures.
    (C) It can be used to lubricate machines.
    (D) It contains caffetannic acids.
    (E) Its stimulating effects make those who drink it feel better.

24. As it is used in the passage, what does the word "principal" (line 40) most nearly mean?

    (A) related to an initial investment
    (B) most important
    (C) with strong opinions
    (D) related to the person who runs a school
    (E) related to moral or ethical standards

25. Which of the following would be the best title for the passage?

    (A) The Universal Appeal of Coffee
    (B) The World's Three Most Popular Beverages
    (C) The Effects of Religious Superstition
    (D) The Stimulating Effects of Caffeine
    (E) The Sense of Smell

Y17HW: Homework and Extra Practice

| SC TOPIC: Analyzing Unknown Words (Lesson Y17a) | RC TOPIC: Inference Questions (Lesson Y16b) |

Homework Set 1

1. Although most of the storm's effects were ------, it did have one positive impact: refilling the city's water reservoir, which had been ------ by a year-long drought.

   (A) auspicious . . aggregated
   (B) detrimental . . depleted
   (C) superfluous . . amplified
   (D) adverse . . augmented
   (E) beneficial . . diminished

2. Many of Mark's classmates were very ambitious, and were applying to medical or law schools, but Mark was ------ with just an undergraduate degree.

   (A) envious
   (B) content
   (C) indifferent
   (D) humiliated
   (E) dejected

3. Joan knew that her chances of winning the singing contest's top prize were ------, but she could not help dreaming about how she would spend the prize money.

   (A) rational
   (B) vindictive
   (C) benign
   (D) credible
   (E) remote

4. The novel was ------ for using too many old-fashioned words, many of which were ------ fifty years before it was published.

   (A) condemned . . evocative
   (B) lauded . . innovative
   (C) salvaged . . conventional
   (D) denounced . . obsolete
   (E) mitigated . . archaic

5. A journalist must know when to reveal information to the public and when to be more ------ so as to prevent embarrassing information from coming to light.

   (A) verbose
   (B) dubious
   (C) discreet
   (D) reckless
   (E) discordant

6. Despite their best efforts, the exterminators were not able to ------ the cockroaches; the pests proved to be more ------ than anyone had expected.

   (A) purge . . transitory
   (B) alleviate . . persistent
   (C) incite . . compliant
   (D) extinguish . . mandatory
   (E) eradicate . . resilient

Unauthorized copying or reuse of any part of this page is illegal.

Homework Set 2

7. A spy must learn to keep two identities: the false one that is revealed to the public and the true one, which must remain ------.

    (A) covert
    (B) congenial
    (C) apparent
    (D) veracious
    (E) remarkable

8. Yolanda was always the most ------ of her siblings, so she was not surprised when they came to her for advice.

    (A) moronic
    (B) prudent
    (C) perplexing
    (D) desolate
    (E) absurd

9. William Shakespeare's ------ works include 38 plays and over 150 sonnets.

    (A) considerate
    (B) voluminous
    (C) transitory
    (D) docile
    (E) frugal

10. Tori's hair was so ------ that it often seemed to completely envelop her head, neck and shoulders.

    (A) confined
    (B) abundant
    (C) petite
    (D) negligible
    (E) ambivalent

11. The ------ actor was becoming nearly as well known for his ------ as for his acting thanks to his numerous charitable projects.

    (A) noteworthy . . maliciousness
    (B) mystical . . conciseness
    (C) prominent . . benevolence
    (D) anonymous . . philanthropy
    (E) humble . . reclusiveness

12. Everett's concern about his test scores proved to be ------, for he received his scores ten minutes later.

    (A) submissive
    (B) pliable
    (C) incredulous
    (D) fleeting
    (E) abiding

Homework Passage 1 (Short Paired)

Passage 1:

On the television show *Star Trek: The Next
Generation*, the character Geordi, who was born blind, is
afforded the ability to see by a "visor" that attaches to his
Line brain. While the show is science fiction and set hundreds
(5) of years in the future, such a revolutionary technology is
not so far-fetched. Over the past few decades, scientists
have been developing brain implants that convert visual
signals into electrical impulses that are used to stimulate
the brain. These implants allow people with acquired
(10) blindness (i.e., those who have been blinded by a disease
or accident) to regain a limited sort of vision. As of yet,
the vision is very limited—black and white, very low
resolution—but patients are able to perform simple visual
tasks. One man even regained the ability to drive a car,
(15) albeit slowly.

Passage 2:

So-called "jetpacks," or rockets designed to allow a
single person to fly without the aid of a vehicle, have
been a mainstay of science fiction since the 1920s. In
Line books, comics, and movies like *The Rocketeer*, jetpacks
(20) allow ordinary citizens to quickly gain the ability to fly
through the air at high speeds for long periods of time. In
the real world, despite much interest from engineers,
jetpacks have had only very limited success.

The first implementation of the jetpack was by
(25) Germany during World War II. The German jetpack was
designed to allow soldiers to "jump" over obstacles like
fences and rivers; its maximum flight time was only a
few seconds, however. Modern jetpacks allow for
somewhat longer flights—up to nine minutes—and can
(30) reach speeds of nearly 80 miles per hour, but they are
extremely expensive and highly dangerous. The day
when everyone will be able to fly to work with their own
jetpack seems to be no nearer than it was 60 years ago.

13. Passage 1 implies that the "brain implants" (line 7)

   (A) are too dangerous and costly to be used on most
   patients.
   (B) cannot be used on patients who were blind at birth.
   (C) are purely fictional.
   (D) have been conceptualized since the 1920s.
   (E) can currently produce blurry color images.

14. Which of the following best states the main idea of Passage
2?

   (A) Jetpacks have yet to be developed into a practical
   everyday technology.
   (B) The jetpack will soon replace the automobile and the
   airplane.
   (C) The idea for jetpacks came from the television show
   Star Trek: The Next Generation.
   (D) Germany's invention of the jetpack helped it achieve
   several victories during World War II.
   (E) Jetpack technology has not advanced at all since World
   War II.

15. Both passages describe inventions that

   (A) are quite practical for most people.
   (B) allow humans to achieve superhuman feats.
   (C) provide a cheap and simple solution to a problem.
   (D) are similar to technologies from science fiction.
   (E) were developed for military use.

16. The attitudes of the authors of the two passages differ in that
the author of Passage 2 is more

   (A) ironic.
   (B) optimistic.
   (C) admiring.
   (D) objective.
   (E) skeptical.

Unauthorized copying or reuse of any part of this page is illegal.

Homework Passage 2 (Short)

Around 15,000 years ago, a lake covered much of what is now Utah. Today, this prehistoric lake is known as Lake Bonneville (after an 18ᵗʰ-century French-
Line American explorer). Lake Bonneville was at one point
(5) more than 1,000 feet deep and more than 20,000 square miles in area—nearly as large as Lake Michigan and much deeper. By around 14,500 years ago, however, the lake had broken through a part of its banks, and most of its water flowed out in a catastrophic flood. During the
(10) flood, a 410-foot-high wall of water rushed at 70 miles per hour across Idaho and Washington. It was probably the second-largest flood in known geologic history. Fortunately, no humans are known to have existed in North America at the time.
(15) All that remains of Lake Bonneville today is a huge dry lakebed and several much smaller lakes, including the Great Salt Lake. To give an idea of how big Lake Bonneville was, the Great Salt Lake is the 37ᵗʰ-largest lake in the world, but it is only about one-twelfth the size
(20) of Lake Bonneville.

17. The primary purpose of the passage is most likely to

(A) describe the discovery of a huge lake by a famous explorer.
(B) detail the damage caused by a natural disaster.
(C) explain why a noteworthy geographical feature no longer exists.
(D) establish the date when humans first colonized North America.
(E) provide a list of the world's deepest lakes.

18. The passage implies that the Great Salt Lake

(A) was formed from the remnants of Lake Bonneville.
(B) is more than 1,000 feet deep.
(C) is the saltiest lake in the world.
(D) is roughly the same size that Lake Bonneville was.
(E) will someday release its water in a huge flood.

Unauthorized copying or reuse of any part of this page is illegal.

Version 1.3

Homework Passage 3 (Long)

The following passage is based on a set of "linguistic auto-biographies" written by college students who did not learn English until moving to America during childhood.

Despite decades of research findings to the contrary, there is still a common belief that bilingualism is bad for children and unpatriotic, and that the only way to be a
Line true American is to leave behind any other language and
(5) allegiance that might be in your background. Children— both long-term Americans and immigrants—often buy into this belief system. At the same time, however, there is a strong feeling among many immigrant families that it is important to preserve ties with the old country and to
(10) maintain their heritage language.

It is usually the goal of the parents for their children to learn English fluently and adapt to their host country but not forget their heritage language. To the parents' disappointment (and ultimately to the regret of the child),
(15) this goal is only rarely fully achieved. It is commonplace for fluency in the first language to decline as English improves, so that by the end of the high school years, children are at best semi-speakers of their heritage language.

(20) The most frequent experience reported by the students in their linguistic autobiographies is that they knew little or no English when they started school in the United States. Many experienced "language shock." As one student reported, "I never expected such difficulties
(25) in assimilating into a brand new culture with a brand new language." None of these students had ever been in a bilingual education program, which suggests that despite all the controversy about bilingual education, true bilingual education programs are rare, at least for Asian
(30) Americans. For some students, however, English as a second language (ESL) classes were available in school.

The autobiographies revealed a hodgepodge of approaches to teaching English. Many schools were inadequately prepared for students who needed to learn
(35) English, and some bizarre solutions were offered at times: "The only [classes] offered to non-English speakers were ESL for Spanish speakers and Sign Language for the deaf. Since I couldn't be put in the ESL classes, I was taught sign language. That was the only
(40) way I knew how to communicate with all the white people who talked so differently than myself. Gradually I began to learn English from my classmates." The other main sources from which students reported learning English were television and friends, but many also
(45) reported that family played a significant role.

Although some students are still struggling to perfect their English in college, most of their worst difficulties with the language are behind them. At this point, most of them are dominant in English, and they find that their
(50) heritage language has suffered. One student reported, "I noticed that I began to think more and more in English. Now, the only thing that is still Chinese in my mind is the multiplication table. I wish I had kept up with my reading skills in Chinese. It felt as though my Chinese

(55) heritage was fading away with my Chinese literacy." First language attrition is discussed in almost everyone's autobiographies.

First language attrition may manifest itself in different ways. Many children, for example, have only a
(60) passive knowledge of their heritage language. They may reach a point at which they understand the home language in a basic way but cannot speak as well as they understand. Others may learn to speak their heritage language fluently but are unable to read and write it.

(65) In other cases, children—and sometimes their parents—speak a mixture of their native language and English. Mixed Korean and English is often called "Konglish," or "Korenglish" as one student prefers to call it—spinoffs on the first word in this genre, "Spanglish."
(70) Sometimes, this mixed language actually becomes the main language used at home. "My family and I still speak more English than Hindi at home. We have even developed a sort of Hinglish, which often consists of a mixture of the two languages." In the majority of cases,
(75) this is done by people who command one language better than the other. Because most of the students who wrote in these autobiographies are only semi-speakers of their heritage language, many report language mixing as the best they can do with their heritage language.

19. The passage implies that many new immigrants experience which of the following conflicts?

(A) the desire to learn a new language *versus* the lack of time needed to do so
(B) racial stereotypes *versus* cultural sensitivity
(C) loyalty to one's new country *versus* the desire to keep one's cultural identity alive
(D) a feeling that bilingualism is beneficial *versus* the results of extensive research
(E) a desire to fit in *versus* a lack of patriotism

20. One can infer that a child who is learning English as a second language will most likely

(A) become skilled in several other languages as well.
(B) maintain fluency in his or her original language.
(C) never fully be able to master English.
(D) avoid mixing the two languages.
(E) gradually become less proficient in his or her original language.

21. What does the term "language shock" (line 23) mean in the context of the passage?

    (A) the realization that one is forgetting his or her original language

    (B) the disappointment parents feel when their children communicate in a mixture of two languages

    (C) unexpected difficulty in adapting to a new culture and a new language

    (D) surprise at finding that English is not very difficult to learn

    (E) the struggles many students have in maintaining fluency in more than one language

22. The passage implies that bilingual education

    (A) has caused much more controversy than actual impact.

    (B) is largely ineffective.

    (C) causes students to have trouble assimilating into American society.

    (D) is unpatriotic.

    (E) creates mixed languages like "Spanglish" and "Konglish."

23. Why was one Asian-American student put in a sign-language class, according to the passage?

    (A) because there were too many students in its English as a Second Language class

    (B) because he was interested in learning sign language

    (C) because the student was mostly deaf

    (D) because the school was unprepared to help non-Spanish-speakers learn English

    (E) because the school had a large population of deaf students

24. The passage cites all of the following methods for learning English EXCEPT

    (A) taking an ESL course

    (B) watching television

    (C) studying English books independently

    (D) learning from friends or classmates

    (E) practicing with family members

25. On the average, the college students who wrote the histories

    (A) were still much more fluent in their first language than in English.

    (B) could speak well in English but not write well.

    (C) were completely bilingual.

    (D) had equal difficulties understanding English and their native tongue.

    (E) were much more fluent in English than in their original language.

26. In context, the word "passive" (line 60) most nearly means

    (A) submissive to the will of others

    (B) completely non-functional

    (C) unemotional

    (D) mentally or physically weak

    (E) able to understand something but not use it

27. Why might a mixed language like "Korenglish" or "Hinglish" become the main language of a household?

    (A) It allows for a smooth transition between two cultures.

    (B) The parents speak English poorly and the children speak the native language poorly.

    (C) The mixed language is the predominant language of a bilingual education program.

    (D) The mixed language can express concepts that neither individual language can express on its own.

    (E) It is the most efficient way to keep both languages alive in the minds of the children.

28. The primary purpose of the passage is to

    (A) illuminate a few of the difficulties facing immigrants whose first language is not English.

    (B) discuss the history of immigrants in America.

    (C) praise Americans who manage to learn a language other than English.

    (D) describe how a typical ESL program operates.

    (E) argue that bilingual education should be banned.

Unauthorized copying or reuse of any part of this page is illegal.   Version 1.3

Y18HW: Homework and Extra Practice

SC Topic: Analyzing Unknown Words (Lesson Y17a) | **RC Topic**: Time Management (Lesson Y18b)

Homework Set 1

1. Millions have seen Nicholas Cage's movies, but only his most ------ fans know that his original last name is "Coppola," not "Cage."

   (A) fervent
   (B) conventional
   (C) covert
   (D) indifferent
   (E) docile

2. Though Mariska was full of ------ about bungee jumping for the first time, she hid her nervousness so well that none of her friends were ------ it.

   (A) assurance . . conscious of
   (B) anxiety . . oblivious to
   (C) distress . . ascribed to
   (D) apprehension . . cognizant of
   (E) pertinence . . perplexed by

3. One of the features of the mansion is a ------ library that includes more than 2,000 books.

   (A) modest
   (B) minute
   (C) deplorable
   (D) futile
   (E) voluminous

4. Xue Ping could not be ------ climbing the world's 10 tallest mountains; he was absolutely ------ in his desire to fulfill this goal.

   (A) obstructed from . . timid
   (B) persuaded to . . persistent
   (C) deterred from . . resolute
   (D) prohibited from . . submissive
   (E) indicted by . . destitute

5. The visitors to the garbage dump were ------ a variety of repulsive odors.

   (A) circumvented by
   (B) commended by
   (C) assailed with
   (D) elated about
   (E) reverted to

6. Roza will not go to the movies tonight because she is unwilling to ------ her parents' order that she stay at home and study.

   (A) defy
   (B) comply with
   (C) concede to
   (D) elicit
   (E) acclaim

 Unauthorized copying or reuse of any part of this page is illegal.

Homework Set 2

7. Although her statements had been proven false by numerous studies, Stephanie refused to ------ her claims; in fact, she reaffirmed their ------.

    (A) retract . . veracity
    (B) convey . . precision
    (C) repudiate . . dubiousness
    (D) accentuate . . accuracy
    (E) acknowledge . . ambiguity

8. The volcano is ------ now, but it was the source of some of the largest eruptions in history when it was active.

    (A) roused
    (B) incensed
    (C) revived
    (D) dormant
    (E) animated

9. Vidya was enjoying the dinner so much that she sought to ------ it by ordering a second dessert.

    (A) compress
    (B) protract
    (C) delegate
    (D) condense
    (E) revoke

10. Some patients who took the medication experienced ------ effects, but all of them reported that it ------ their pain, and most wished to continue taking it.

    (A) amiable . . depleted
    (B) adverse . . alleviated
    (C) detrimental . . incited
    (D) conducive . . mitigated
    (E) benign . . denounced

11. Tibor was ------ in his refusal, clearly stating that he would not sing in front of others, not even for a million dollars.

    (A) evasive
    (B) unequivocal
    (C) opaque
    (D) ambivalent
    (E) discreet

12. The formerly wealthy athlete was forced to ------ his house when he could no longer afford to pay for it.

    (A) acquire
    (B) attain
    (C) abide in
    (D) aggregate
    (E) relinquish

Unauthorized copying or reuse of any part of this page is illegal.

Homework Passage 1 (Short)

Have you ever wondered why golf balls have
dimples? Many people assume that a smooth ball would
travel farther and more reliably than a ball with many
Line little indentations in it. This, however, does not fit with
(5) the laws of aerodynamics. As a ball travels through air, it
is surrounded by a thin layer of stationary air. The
dimples on a golf ball allow this air layer to stay intact
for longer, thus protecting the ball from higher pressures.
Since higher pressures create air resistance (or "drag"), a
(10) ball that lacks dimples will slow down more quickly, and
travel more erratically, than a dimpled ball.

Similar forces explain how baseballs (with their
raised seams) can be made to curve through air.

13. The passage states that "golf balls have dimples" (lines 1-2)
because

(A) dimpled balls are cheaper to produce than smooth balls.
(B) the dimples reduce the air resistance on the ball.
(C) the air layer surrounding a ball is disrupted by dimples.
(D) dimples lower the mass of the ball.
(E) the dimples allow the ball to curve while in the air.

14. The primary purpose of the passage is to

(A) prove that smooth golf balls can be aimed more reliably
than dimpled ones.
(B) explain a common phenomenon.
(C) describe the rules of golf.
(D) compare golf and baseball.
(E) show how car manufacturers reduce air resistance on
their vehicles.

Homework Passage 2 (Short)

The earliest ancestor of the bicycle was invented in
1818 by a German named Karl Drais. Dubbed the
Laufmaschine ("running machine"), it was the first
Line personal vehicle to utilize a two-wheeled design. Its
(5) similarities to modern bicycles more or less end there,
however. The *Laufmaschine* (also called a "dandy horse"
due to its popularity with "dandies," or fashionable
young men) had no pedals; to cause it to move forward,
its rider pushed off the ground with his or her feet, as if
(10) running. As you might expect, this led to safety issues,
particularly when the dandy horse was used in pedestrian
areas. Many countries banned its use in public, and after
only a year of popularity, the device faded into obscurity.

It was not for another 40 years that a group of
(15) Frenchmen created the modern pedal-powered design,
which they called a "velocipede." Many different
versions of the velocipede were sold, including the
ridiculous bicycles known as "penny-farthings," which
had a pathetically tiny back wheel and a huge front
(20) wheel, with the rider perched precariously on top.

15. The passage implies that many countries banned the
Laufmaschine because it

(A) looked ridiculous.
(B) was popular with "dandies."
(C) caused damage to city streets.
(D) posed a threat to the safety of pedestrians.
(E) was expensive and inefficient.

16. The author's attitude toward "penny-farthings" (line 18) is
most nearly one of

(A) awe.
(B) longing.
(C) disinterest.
(D) mockery.
(E) appreciation.

 Unauthorized copying or reuse of any part of this page is illegal.

Homework Passage 3 (Short)

The modern borders between nations are often based on natural geographic features (such as coastlines, rivers, and mountains). Sometimes, they are the product of
Line large-scale wars; more rarely, they are formed when huge
(5) kingdoms are peacefully subdivided.

One example of this latter case is the heart of Western Europe, including modern-day France and Germany, as well as the smaller countries that lie between them. In the 8th and 9th centuries A.D., the
(10) Frankish king Charlemagne conquered nearly all of Western Europe. After the death of Charlemagne's son, King Louis the Pious, there was a great dispute between Louis' three surviving sons over who would rule the kingdom. In 843, rather than go to war, the brothers
(15) forged the Treaty of Verdun: Charles the Bald would receive the western portion, which became the nation of France; Louis the German received the eastern portion, which became (you guessed it) Germany; and Lothair received the middle territories, which became northern
(20) Italy, Switzerland, Belgium, and the Netherlands.

17. One can infer from information in the passage that most countries' borders are based on

(A) natural geography.
(B) religion.
(C) ethnicity.
(D) military conquest.
(E) peaceful agreements.

18. In context, "forged" (line 15) most nearly means

(A) falsified.
(B) heated.
(C) created.
(D) hammered.
(E) copied.

Homework Passage 4 (Long)

The following is adapted from an article by a man who (along with his wife) volunteered in the remote mountain village of Maimafu, in Papua New Guinea.

Maimafu was a preserved example of communal living. Men rallied to the building of a new home, the elderly worked and lived with their families, and mothers
Line breast-fed their neighbors' children. In fact, the one
(5) parentless, Down's syndrome man in our village was fed, housed, and clothed by everyone; he would spend a few days with one family before happily wandering in to work or play with the next.

It was when we had settled in that it happened. We
(10) were sitting in a circle on the ground with a large group of villagers to "tok stori," Papua New Guinea's favorite pastime of "telling stories." I had passed around photos I had snapped back home in Chicago. A villager was staring intently at one of the photos. He had spotted two
(15) homeless men on a Michigan Avenue sidewalk with crude signs propped between their legs.

"Tupela man wokem wanem?" he asked. ("What are these two men doing?")

I attempted to explain the concept of homelessness
(20) to the group, and the desire of these two men to get some food. Crowding around the photograph for a good stare, the villagers could not comprehend how the men became homeless, or why the passersby in the photo were so indifferent. They bombarded me with questions and I did
(25) my best to make sense of the two ragged beggars in the midst of such glittering skyscrapers. I read from their questions and solemn mood that they had made an important observation—these two men must lack not only food and shelter but also a general sense of affection
(30) and purpose in their community.

Early the next morning, we were startled to hear a sharp rap at the door. Opening it, I was greeted by Moia, Kabarae, Kavalo, and Lemek. My wife and I went out into the bright, beautiful day and sat with them in a
(35) circle. Each man gave us a pineapple. Moia spoke: "After you left last night, all of us men on the village council had a very big meeting. For a long, long time we discussed the two men in your picture. We have reached a conclusion and have a proposal for you."
(40) "What could this possibly be?" we wondered.

"Please contact those two men as well as your government. Ask the government if they will fly those two men to Maimafu, just like they did for you. We have marked two spots of land where we will build houses for
(45) those two men, just like we built for you. Our men will build the houses and the women will plant the gardens to feed them."

They were offering to do what? I was stunned and overwhelmed. Their offer was bold and genuine. It was
(50) innocent and naive. It was beautiful. And, like the twist of a kaleidoscope, my worldview had changed.

What does one say to such an offer? We stammered for a response and stumbled over explanations of difficult logistics, scarce money, and government bureaucracies.

(55) But the councilmen would not accept no for an answer. In their simple lives, it was impossible to comprehend that humanity was host to such an injustice.

The villagers were serious. They were offering everything they had. We reluctantly matched their
(60) enthusiasm with a few letters to America and long conversations with the village council. We toured the sites where the homes were to be built. We listened to the women discuss the type of gardens they would plant, which would even include coffee trees to generate a
(65) small income. The plan could not work, we told them. Their hearts sank, and I could see in their eyes that this dream would not die easily.

"Sori tru, sori tru we no inap wokem dospela samting," they told us. ("We are sorry this can't happen.")
(70) They clicked their tongues and shook their heads in disappointment.

Initially inspired by the episode, I begin mulling questions over and over in my mind. I would think of the spiritual wealth of Maimafu and the material wealth of
(75) America: Can a community reach a balance of material wealth and spiritual wealth? Why do these two societies exhibit so much of one and not much of the other? How has the world evolved so that some people own mansions and others lack shoes? How many people have love in
(80) their souls but diseased water in their drinking cups?

19. In what way is Maimafu "a preserved example of communal living" (lines 1-2)?

(A) Everyone in the village lives in the same large house.
(B) The village relies on food and tools sent from other villages in Papua New Guinea.
(C) The villagers help each other and share their possessions when needed.
(D) No one in the village can do anything until the entire village approves.
(E) The villagers worship nature and speak to their gods frequently.

20. The treatment of the "Down's syndrome man" (line 5) reveals what important quality of the village?

(A) that some members of the village are sad and unsatisfied
(B) that everyone shares burdens so that no one suffers too much and everyone has what they need
(C) that the village has poor medical care
(D) that no member of the village wants to care for the man for more than a few days
(E) that genetic conditions exist in greater proportion in the village than elsewhere

21. Why did the villager stare at the picture of the two men on Michigan Avenue?

   (A) He could not believe that people in America could be so lazy.
   (B) He wanted to own an outfit like the ones the men were wearing.
   (C) He was in awe of the tall, shiny buildings.
   (D) He could not figure out why they were sitting on the street with signs between their legs.
   (E) He wondered why they were not in a homeless shelter.

22. The passage implies that the villagers "could not comprehend" homelessness because

   (A) the homeless people in their village were in much poorer condition than those in Chicago.
   (B) they blamed the men in the picture for not doing more to help themselves.
   (C) they did not understand English.
   (D) there was no such thing as a homeless person in their society.
   (E) they were uneducated and naïve.

23. In line 32, the word "rap" most nearly means

   (A) quick knocking sound
   (B) prison sentence
   (C) informal discussion
   (D) harsh criticism
   (E) musical style featuring rhymed, spoken vocals

24. What was the "proposal" (line 39) of the village council?

   (A) to bring the homeless men to the village, build them houses, and help to feed them
   (B) to teach the American government how to have a village with no homelessness
   (C) to donate a few pineapples to the homeless men so that they could eat
   (D) to teach the men in the picture how to farm and hunt
   (E) to travel to Chicago and help build the men new houses

25. The passage implies that the narrator's "worldview had changed" (line 51) because

   (A) he had spent too much time playing with his kaleidoscope.
   (B) the homeless men preferred Papua New Guinea to America
   (C) he had realized that Maimafu was a wealthier place than Chicago
   (D) the villagers' generous offer had made him re-evaluate his acceptance of America's social values.
   (E) he had previously thought of the villagers as being selfish and dishonest.

26. The passage implies that the villagers' motivation in making their proposal is to

   (A) increase the size and wealth of their village.
   (B) make friends with more Americans.
   (C) criticize the narrator and his wife.
   (D) show the Americans that their village is superior to American cities.
   (E) end an injustice.

27. The questions in the final paragraph (lines 75-80) point out the contrast between

   (A) some villagers' generosity and other villagers' selfishness.
   (B) the narrator's wealth and the homeless men's poverty.
   (C) the sizes of different houses in Maimafu.
   (D) the cost of shoes and pineapples in America and in Papua New Guinea
   (E) communities with lots of money and possessions and communities that care for their citizens.

28. The primary purpose of the passage is to

   (A) praise Americans for building "glittering skyscrapers."
   (B) chronicle the history of the village of Maimafu.
   (C) tell a story that illuminates a key difference between two cultures.
   (D) describe the geography of Papua New Guinea.
   (E) criticize Americans for not doing more to prevent homelessness.

Unauthorized copying or reuse of any part of this page is illegal.

Version 1.3

SC Topic: Guessing and Review (Lesson Y19a)	RC Topic: Time Management (Lesson Y18b)

Homework Set 1

1. Hera had many questions about the topics discussed in the meeting, but she chose to save them for later rather than to ------ the meeting and waste other people's time.

   (A) protract
   (B) revert
   (C) hasten
   (D) accelerate
   (E) eradicate

2. Gerald would not ------ the plan until he received assurances that it would not exceed his company's budget.

   (A) endorse
   (B) ascribe
   (C) relinquish
   (D) deplore
   (E) revoke

3. When he discovered that his neighbors were too ------ about crime, Mr. Sullivan tried to ------ them from their unworried state so that they would join his neighborhood watch group.

   (A) content . . dwindle
   (B) perturbed . . rouse
   (C) complacent . . incite
   (D) dissenting . . hibernate
   (E) indiscreet . . recede

4. One cautious step at a time, Annette ------ walked across the tightrope.

   (A) evocatively
   (B) tentatively
   (C) inexplicably
   (D) assertively
   (E) abundantly

5. The ------ of the lion is nearly unmatched among land carnivores; it consumes up to 15 pounds of meat a day.

   (A) prudence
   (B) dormancy
   (C) apprehension
   (D) voracity
   (E) submissiveness

6. As a mediator, it was Brenda's job to ensure that each negotiation went smoothly and ------, and that each side came away thinking that the agreement was ------.

   (A) contemptuously . . just
   (B) concisely . . cowardly
   (C) congenially . . destitute
   (D) covertly . . provincial
   (E) cordially . . equitable

Unauthorized copying or reuse of any part of this page is illegal.

C2 education
be smarter.

Homework Set 2

7. The train's movement was ------ by the trees that had been knocked onto the tracks by the ------ wind conditions caused by the storm.

    (A) hindered . . auspicious
    (B) circumvented . . intricate
    (C) alleviated . . effusive
    (D) sustained . . fervent
    (E) impeded . . turbulent

8. After seeing the magician seemingly levitate 10 feet off the ground, Marnie was ------; she knew that there was a hidden device lifting the performer.

    (A) gullible
    (B) obsolete
    (C) incredulous
    (D) pliable
    (E) dejected

9. In an effort to ------ the ------ man, the police officer used a calm tone of voice and reminded the man that if he continued his hostile behavior, he would be arrested.

    (A) placate . . belligerent
    (B) appease . . commendable
    (C) refute . . contentious
    (D) reconcile . . tranquil
    (E) assail . . docile

10. When asked what he wanted to eat for dinner, Juan offered only ------ answers, so his wife chose the restaurant herself.

    (A) definitive
    (B) conducive
    (C) beneficial
    (D) equivocal
    (E) resolute

11. Though she considered the play to be juvenile and pointless, Julia chose not to ------ it in public, because she was friends with the director and did not want to hurt his feelings.

    (A) laud
    (B) deride
    (C) savor
    (D) retain
    (E) venerate

12. In an attempt to ------ the damage done by the flu outbreak, the mayor ordered that all schools be closed so that children would not be exposed to the virus.

    (A) incense
    (B) comply with
    (C) esteem
    (D) persist
    (E) mitigate

Unauthorized copying or reuse of any part of this page is illegal.

Version 1.3

Homework Passage 1 (Short Paired)

Passage 1:

How did a nation that is over 80% covered with glaciers come to be called "Greenland"? The legend is that the original Norse settler, Erik the Red, was expelled
Line from Iceland for the crime of murder. Upon settling in
(5) the new land to the west, which was far icier and far less green than Iceland, Erik sought to attract more settlers to his new community. He supposedly then named the new area "Greenland," thinking that such an enticing name would ensure the success of the venture. While the
(10) settlement lasted for over four centuries, it died out sometime in the 15th century, probably from malnutrition and disease.

Another possibility is that Erik meant to name the land "Gruntland" ("Ground-land"), but that this was
(15) erroneously changed to "Groenland" ("Green-land"). In Norse, "grunt" could also refer to a shallow bay, a geographical feature that is plentiful in Greenland.

Passage 2:

The world's largest island (not counting continents)
Line is also a land of paradoxes. This country calls itself
(20) Greenland, but is probably the coldest, iciest, and—let's be honest—least green nation on Earth. It claims independence but is also considered a part of the Kingdom of Denmark. It is one of the largest countries by land area but one of the smallest by population, with
(25) fewer than 60,000 people spread out over the few livable areas (mainly along the western coast) of the gargantuan, 800,000-plus square mile island. By way of comparison, there are over 500 *cities* in America alone with a greater population. To put it another way, if Greenland were as
(30) densely populated as the state of New York, it would have over 340 million inhabitants (more than the current population of the United States).

13. One can infer from information in Passage 1 that its author most likely believes that

(A) Erik the Red was innocent of murder.
(B) Iceland is a less pleasant place to live than Greenland.
(C) "Gruntland" would be a more appropriate name than "Greenland."
(D) Greenland has a plentiful supply of farmland and fish.
(E) Greenland should declare its independence from Denmark.

14. What information in Passage 1 best explains the statement in Passage 2 that Greenland "has fewer than 60,000 people spread out over the few livable areas" (lines 25-26)?

(A) Shallow bays, or "grunts," are "plentiful in Greenland" (line 17).
(B) Erik the Red "was expelled from Iceland for the crime of murder" (lines 3-4).
(C) The original Greenland settlement "lasted for over four centuries" (line 10).
(D) Erik the Red "sought to attract more settlers" to Greenland (line 6).
(E) Greenland "is over 80% covered with glaciers" (lines 1-2).

15. Both passages mention which fact about Greenland?

(A) It has little plant life but lots of ice.
(B) It is the world's largest island.
(C) It has many shallow bays.
(D) It was founded by Erik the Red.
(E) It has a very small population.

16. The primary distinction between the passages is that Passage 1 focuses more on

(A) comparing Greenland to other countries.
(B) the sparseness of Greenland's population.
(C) listing the largest countries in the world by area.
(D) Greenland's many contradictions.
(E) the origin of the name "Greenland."

Unauthorized copying or reuse of any part of this page is illegal.

Homework Passage 2 (Short)

Two of the most prolific inventors of all time, Thomas Edison and Nikola Tesla, were also bitter rivals. Edison, whose inventions include the electric light bulb
Line and the kinetoscope (an early motion picture camera),
(5) hired Tesla when the latter first came to America. Their partnership quickly dissolved due to disputes over work styles and payments, causing Tesla to strike out on his own. Soon afterward, their dispute grew to such levels that it captured the attention of the world.

(10) At the heart of this conflict was the debate over which system the country should adopt for transferring power from generating stations to individual homes and businesses. Edison's claimed that his "direct current" (DC) model was safer and more powerful than the
(15) "alternating current" (AC) model invented by Tesla. Tesla in turn pointed out that his AC system was able to transmit energy efficiently across hundreds of miles (compared to only a couple miles for DC). Ultimately, Edison's claims were proven to be inaccurate, and
(20) Tesla's AC system became the dominant form of power transmission.

17. As it is used in the passage, the phrase "strike out" (line 7) most nearly means

    (A) fail.
    (B) attack.
    (C) embark.
    (D) cancel.
    (E) draw a line through.

18. The passage implies that which of the following statements regarding the resolution of "the debate" (line 10) is true?

    (A) Both systems proved equally effective at transmitting power.
    (B) Most power systems began using alternating current.
    (C) Tesla's company bought Edison's invention and implemented it across the country.
    (D) Edison and Tesla resolved their differences and became friends.
    (E) Edison's system won out despite being technically inferior.

Homework Passage 3 (Long)

This passage is an excerpt from the beginning of Charlotte Brontë's 1853 novel, Vilette.

My godmother lived in a handsome house in the clean and ancient town of Bretton. Her husband's family had been residents there for generations, and bore,
Line indeed, the name of their birthplace—Bretton of Bretton:
(5) whether by coincidence, or because some remote ancestor had been a personage of sufficient importance to leave his name to his neighbourhood, I know not.

When I was a girl I went to Bretton about twice a year, and well I liked the visit. The house and its inmates
(10) specially suited me. The large peaceful rooms, the well-arranged furniture, the clear wide windows, the balcony outside, looking down on a fine antique street, where Sundays and holidays seemed always to abide—so quiet was its atmosphere, so clean its pavement—these things
(15) pleased me well.

One child in a household of grown people is usually made very much of, and in a quiet way I was a good deal taken notice of by Mrs. Bretton, who had been left a widow, with one son, before I knew her; her husband, a
(20) physician, having died while she was yet a young and handsome woman.

She was not young, as I remember her, but she was still handsome, tall, well-made, and though dark for an Englishwoman, yet wearing always the clearness of
(25) health in her brunette cheek, and its vivacity in a pair of fine, cheerful black eyes. People esteemed it a grievous pity that she had not conferred her complexion on her son, whose eyes were blue—though, even in boyhood, very piercing—and the colour of his long hair such as
(30) friends did not venture to specify, except as the sun shone on it, when they called it golden. He inherited the lines of his mother's features, however; also her good teeth, her stature (or the promise of her stature, for he was not yet full-grown), and, what was better, her health
(35) without flaw, and her spirits of that tone and equality which are better than a fortune to the possessor.

In the autumn of the year 1840 I was staying at Bretton; my godmother having come in person to claim me of the kinsfolk with whom was at that time fixed my
(40) permanent residence. I believe she then plainly saw events coming, whose very shadow I scarce guessed; yet of which the faint suspicion sufficed to impart unsettled sadness, and made me glad to change scene and society.

Time always flowed smoothly for me at my
(45) godmother's side; not with tumultuous swiftness, but blandly, like the gliding of a full river through a plain. My visits to her resembled the sojourn of Christian and Hopeful beside a certain pleasant stream, with "green trees on each bank, and meadows beautified with lilies all
(50) the year round." The charm of variety there was not, nor the excitement of incident; but I liked peace so well, and sought stimulus so little, that when the latter came I almost felt it a disturbance, and wished rather it had still held aloof.

Unauthorized copying or reuse of any part of this page is illegal.

Version 1.3

19. Why does the narrator say that "Sundays and holidays seemed always to abide" (line 13) in the streets of Bretton?

    (A) The town seemed to always be relaxed and old-fashioned.
    (B) The citizens of Bretton were extremely religious.
    (C) No one lived in the town.
    (D) The townsfolk were extremely lazy.
    (E) Many people always crowded the streets outside her godmother's house.

20. According to the passage, why does Mrs. Bretton pay attention to the narrator?

    (A) Mrs. Bretton had never married or had children.
    (B) The narrator looked exactly like Mrs. Bretton.
    (C) There were no other children in the household.
    (D) The narrator was the loudest and most cheerful person in the house.
    (E) Mrs. Bretton was very concerned about the narrator's lack of ambition and education.

21. Which of the following best describes the appearance of the narrator's godmother?

    (A) pale-skinned, and sickly looking
    (B) cheerful but ugly
    (C) short and angry
    (D) healthy and blue-eyed
    (E) tall and attractive

22. The son of the narrator's godmother inherited all of the following traits from his mother EXCEPT

    (A) her dark skin and eye color.
    (B) her good health.
    (C) her height.
    (D) her facial features.
    (E) her calm, cheerful manner.

23. In line 39, the word "fixed" most nearly means

    (A) repaired
    (B) influenced dishonestly
    (C) blamed
    (D) set up
    (E) concentrated

24. The last sentence of the passage (lines 50-54) implies that the narrator's peaceful life at Bretton

    (A) would be a permanent aspect of her life.
    (B) was about to become even more relaxing.
    (C) was harmful to her well-being.
    (D) would not last for much longer.
    (E) was unpleasant and boring.

25. The passage is primarily concerned with

    (A) telling the history of the town of Bretton.
    (B) arguing that children should always be surrounded by adults.
    (C) describing the circumstances and the important figures of her childhood.
    (D) criticizing the narrator's godmother for being too harsh and unforgiving.
    (E) comparing the narrator's mother and godmother.

Y20HW: Homework and Extra Practice

SC Topic: Guessing and Review (Lesson Y19a)	**RC Topic**: Time Management (Lesson Y18b)

Homework Set 1

1. Normally a quiet, reserved person, Antoine became ------ and animated whenever he discussed robotics.

    (A) transitory
    (B) desolate
    (C) concise
    (D) effusive
    (E) prudent

2. In contrast to the United States' all-volunteer army, military service is ------ for all healthy males in some countries.

    (A) compulsory
    (B) negligible
    (C) deliberate
    (D) complimentary
    (E) inexplicable

3. The early cellular phone was innovative at the time it was manufactured in 1986, but today it is so bulky and hard to use that it is completely ------.

    (A) prominent
    (B) covert
    (C) mandatory
    (D) outmoded
    (E) extensive

4. The two sides had drastically different views of the judge's ruling; one considered it to be ------ and admirable, while the other thought it was completely unfair and even ------.

    (A) objective . . laudable
    (B) biased . . vile
    (C) unjust . . cordial
    (D) equitable . . repugnant
    (E) ambivalent . . auspicious

5. The debater's arguments were so reasonable and well-supported that his opponent was completely unable to ------ them.

    (A) endorse
    (B) assert
    (C) refute
    (D) alleviate
    (E) concede

6. A majority of voters favored the proposed law, but many of them offered only ------ support for it; by contrast, many of the law's detractors were quite ------ opposed to it.

    (A) intemperate . . eccentrically
    (B) tepid . . fervently
    (C) submissive . . benignly
    (D) mild . . indifferently
    (E) desirous . . enthusiastically

Unauthorized copying or reuse of any part of this page is illegal.

Version 1.3

Homework Set 2

7. After waking from the surgery, Connie felt sore and ------, though the doctors assured her that both the pain and tiredness would ------ in time.

   (A) lively . . multiply
   (B) lethargic . . diminish
   (C) industrious . . wane
   (D) sluggish . . magnify
   (E) elusive . . deteriorate

8. The general was known for his ------ actions; he seemed incapable of caution or uncertainty.

   (A) superfluous
   (B) docile
   (C) decisive
   (D) tentative
   (E) conducive

9. Her bosses considered Leslie to be the ideal employee: uncomplaining, ------, and capable.

   (A) malicious
   (B) transitory
   (C) reclusive
   (D) contemptuous
   (E) diligent

10. The "No Trespassing" signs did little to ------ people from entering the woods on the Patels' property, so they added a barbed-wire fence.

    (A) ascribe
    (B) incite
    (C) deter
    (D) reconcile
    (E) delegate

11. Though Mimi had every right to be bitter about the way she had been treated, her tone was forgiving rather than ------.

    (A) pertinent
    (B) acerbic
    (C) merciful
    (D) dejected
    (E) sympathetic

12. Harold was ------ that some people had evil intentions, but he was still shocked to realize that his cousin had committed such a ------ act.

    (A) incensed . . congenial
    (B) elated . . repulsive
    (C) complacent . . conventional
    (D) cognizant . . malevolent
    (E) naive . . beneficial

Unauthorized copying or reuse of any part of this page is illegal.

Homework Passage 1 (Short)

For over two thousand years, humans have used reflective surfaces to focus the sun's rays. Glass or metal mirrors, when properly arranged, allow sunlight to be
Line focused to a tiny point, which can cause extreme heat at
(5) the receiving end of the ray. Curving the mirrors allows for an even more precise focusing of the solar rays. If a large enough ray targets a wooden object for long enough, the wood begins to smolder and can even catch fire.
(10) Over 2,200 years ago, the famed mathematician and inventor Archimedes supposedly used mirrors to focus sunlight on ships that were attacking his home city of Syracuse (on the isle of Sicily). According to the story, the attacking ships were quickly destroyed (though
(15) Syracuse was eventually captured anyway, and Archimedes was killed during the invasion). While this story may be spurious, modern re-creations have experienced success in setting objects on fire at moderate distances. One group even managed to nearly duplicate
(20) Archimedes' feat: at 100 meters, they caused a ship to smoke and smolder (though not catch fire) using mirrors.

13. According to the story reported in the passage, what was the end result of Archimedes's attempt to use "mirrors to focus sunlight on ships" (lines 11-12)?

    (A) Archimedes' city experienced absolute and lasting triumph.
    (B) The mirrors proved useless because the sky over Syracuse was cloudy.
    (C) One of the attacking ships was sunk, but most of them survived.
    (D) Syracuse won a short-lived victory over their attackers.
    (E) The weapon made the ships smolder but caused little real damage.

14. The author's attitude toward "the story" (line 13) can best be described as

    (A) reasonably skeptical.
    (B) enthusiastically curious.
    (C) utterly furious.
    (D) cruelly mocking.
    (E) wholly trusting.

Homework Passage 2 (Short)

What is the earliest human artwork? While it is impossible to say for sure, we do know that humans have been doing art for at least 35,000 to 40,000 years. Early
Line humans in this era began carving exaggerated female
(5) figures known as "Venuses." The oldest known example, the Venus of Hohle Fels, was found in a German cave in 2008. It was likely worn as a pendant and used in rituals involving fertility. Similar figures of women have been found in many places throughout Europe.
(10) Around 30,000 years ago, humans began creating other types of art, including cave paintings (such as the famous ones at Lascaux, France) and jewelry.
Humans of this era were not limited to the visual arts—flutes dating back at least 35,000 years have been
(15) discovered. In addition to playing musical instruments, early humans almost certainly used their voices to create music (in other words, they sang). It is of course impossible to find archaeological evidence of songs, though, so we'll never know when humans began to sing.

15. The passage implies that the "Venus of Hohle Fels" (line 6)

    (A) was used as a musical instrument.
    (B) is a realistic portrait of an actual woman.
    (C) is certainly the first human artwork ever created.
    (D) had ceremonial as well as decorative functions.
    (E) is unlike other archeological finds from that region.

16. The primary purpose of the passage is to

    (A) compare early human customs from present-day Germany and France.
    (B) provide examples of the earliest known instances of various art forms.
    (C) explain why archeological findings are difficult to date precisely.
    (D) establish the date of the first human song.
    (E) describe the cave paintings of Lascaux.

Unauthorized copying or reuse of any part of this page is illegal.   Version 1.3

Homework Passage 3 (Short)

In Greek mythology, the Amazons were a tribe of fierce female warriors who shunned the contact of men. The original Amazons supposedly hailed from Eastern
Line Europe, most likely from Turkey. They appear in
(5) Homer's *Iliad*, fighting on the side of the city of Troy.

So how did an element from Greek mythology become associated with the South American river of the same name? The river was discovered and mapped mostly by Spanish and Portuguese conquistadors. These
(10) explorers and conquerors initially gave the river several much more descriptive names: *Rio Grande* (Big River), *Mar Dulce* (Sweet Sea, after its huge freshwater estuary), and *Rio de Canela* (Cinnamon River, after cinnamon-like plants that grew along its shores). The first European to
(15) complete a full descent of the river, the Spaniard Francisco de Orellana, was frequently attacked by fierce indigenous female warriors. When the Spanish king, Charles I, heard Orellana's stories, he named the river after the Amazon warriors of legend, and the name stuck.

17. According to the passage, the Amazon River was named by

(A) Homer, author of the *Iliad*.
(B) a Portuguese conquistador.
(C) a Spanish explorer.
(D) a Native American tribe.
(E) a Spanish King.

18. The primary purpose of the passage is to

(A) chronicle the first explorations of the Amazon River.
(B) tease King Charles I for his poor understanding of geography.
(C) clarify the origin of an odd place name.
(D) argue that an ancient Turkish warrior race migrated to the Amazon basin.
(E) catalogue the plant life of the Amazon rainforest.

Homework Passage 4 (Long)

This passage describes the conditions in a small village in the African nation of Mali, which has been afflicted with droughts in recent decades due to climate change.

It is May in Mali, and the rains have not yet come. It is over 115 degrees Fahrenheit and my friend looks up at the sky. We have all been watching the sky for weeks.
Line The spreading desert and the receding grasses in Mali are
(5) causing the rains to arrive later and later every year. My friend looks up once again and says to me with utter acceptance: "We think that it may be Allah's will that we die now."

The next day we watch and wait. Nothing matters at
(10) this point except that the rains come. Everyone is ready to begin plowing the fields, but nothing can be done until it rains. We continue to watch and wait.

A faint wind slips by me. I look up yet again toward the hills in the direction of the wind and I see a few
(15) clouds beginning to blow over them. There is a huge break in the tension of the village as the clouds move in.

The wind begins to blow strong. Bright fabrics blow out from the bodies of the women, dancing and slapping in the air. We all lean against the winds and head for
(20) cover, except for the children, who run frantically toward the giant mango trees. Small mangoes fall from the upper branches and the kids race to collect them in their shirts.

Soon darkness covers us and the rain begins to fall, frantic from the wait. It feels as if the energy of the
(25) weeks before has built up in these clouds—as if they had been forced to hold their breath for weeks and now it has all broken loose. The wind blows branches out of the trees and the rain falls with the fury of a hurricane.

After about an hour, the rain calms and continues
(30) falling throughout the night.

The village will live.

The next day the men begin working acres of fields with steer and an antiquated plow. The women wake early to prepare lunch. It is made from the corn of the
(35) year before. They put the lunch in bowls and balance the bowls on their heads; most have a baby tied with a cloth to their back. They head for the fields. They will do this nearly every day for the next four to five months. Wake early, prepare lunch over a fire, and walk barefoot or in
(40) flip-flops to the fields with a child on their back.

When the fields are ready to plant, the men and women of the village will take a tool made of a wooden handle with a flattened piece of metal attached to the end and they will bend over the earth using only this simple
(45) tool for hours and hours every day.

Within this daily work to sustain life itself, there is a peace, a connection, and a tradition of laughter and music that makes the Malian culture one of happiness and richness.
(50) There are five main family groups that make up my village. Mine is the Wattara family. Each Sunday all of the men in the family work in the same field together. They line up and work side by side, efficiently moving down the rows. The women prepare lunch, care for the

Version 1.3

Unauthorized copying or reuse of any part of this page is illegal.

(55) children, and also labor in the fields on these days.

These are the women who send out the laughter and the music in the fields. These are the women who hold the secrets of the village, the secrets that the world is desperately in search of. The secret of how to make *(60)* music out of toil and how to laugh in the face of hardship and death.

19. Which of the following would make the best title for the passage?

(A) The Politics of Mali
(B) Comedy in Africa
(C) How to Farm in the Desert
(D) Global Warming: Fact or Fiction?
(E) Toiling and Laughing in the Face of Hardship

20. The passage implies that the rains come to Mali later and later each year because

(A) the spreading desert has reduced the amount of water in the atmosphere.
(B) there is too much pollution in the village.
(C) the rain is not needed until mid-summer.
(D) the villagers have displeased Allah.
(E) the weather patterns of the region are temporarily drier, but will soon be reversed.

21. In line 13, the word "faint" most nearly means

(A) dizzy
(B) frantic
(C) barely noticeable
(D) deceptive
(E) unconscious

22. What causes "a huge break in the tension of the village" (lines 15-16)?

(A) mangoes falling from a tree
(B) a solemn acceptance that death is near.
(C) the sight of women preparing a hearty lunch
(D) the first appearance of the rain clouds
(E) the natural happiness of the Malian people.

23. According to the passage, the rain falls

(A) lightly and for several days.
(B) intermittently for a few hours.
(C) only in the neighboring villages.
(D) fiercely at first, then calmly for the rest of the night.
(E) for only a few minutes.

24. The equipment that the villagers use to work their farmland can best be described as

(A) expensive and brand-new
(B) complicated and frequently broken
(C) aged but highly efficient
(D) automated and unfamiliar
(E) simple and old-fashioned

25. How does Malian culture respond to hardship, according to the passage?

(A) with joy and laughter
(B) by despairing
(C) with rational critique
(D) with prayer and ritual
(E) by giving up

26. The primary purpose of the passage is to

(A) contrast the weather of the summer and winter seasons in Mali.
(B) compare the religious practices of various tribes in northern Africa.
(C) describe the members of the Wattara family.
(D) summarize the agricultural methods of an isolated tribe.
(E) show how a small village copes with the threat of its own destruction.

Unauthorized copying or reuse of any part of this page is illegal.   Version 1.3

23115833R00063

Made in the USA
Middletown, DE
19 August 2015